Servant|Marriage

Douglas Weiss, Ph.D.

Servant Marriage
© 2015 1st Editon
by Douglas Weiss, Ph.D.

Published by Discovery Press
P.O. Box 51055
Colorado Springs, CO 80949
719-278-3708

Interior and Cover design by: Janelle Evangelides
Edited by: Jim Kochenburger at Christianwriterhelp.com
Printed in the United States of America

Table of Contents

Introduction

Servant Marriage is a response to the calling we all already received the moment we said, "I do." All the courting, dating, emotional intimacy, quality time, and resources culminated into the primary lifelong relationship we call marriage.

For some, years or decades may have passed since they received their calling to be married to the one with whom they would be given the privilege of serving alongside on their journey called life. However, in current culture, many couples are getting a quite different result from the *happily ever after* we have all heard about. Some feel alone or merely tolerated in marriage. Others feel unappreciated or exploited. Still others feel stuck or trapped "until death do us part." Marriage challenges Christians, and some do not make it—their marriages end in divorce.

How is it that so many start the race of marriage, but growing numbers of them do not cross the finish line of "until death do us part"? As a Christian counselor working with couples in distress for more than a quarter of a century now, I think I have learned quite a bit as I watched brave couples address their wounds, bad ideas, unproductive practices and attitudes, and move toward picking up new ideas to change their marriages for the better.

One of these new ideas is learning that they are servants in their marriage and are responsible for how they believe and behave, and that they will stand before the Lord and give an account of how well they served their spouse—not how well they got served.

Sometimes it helps to start something new with the end in mind. In the end, I will be accountable to God for how I served my wife. I believe this is a major evaluation point for my whole life. It is as if, in my spirit, I know that one of the major questions in heaven will be, "How well did you treat my daughter, Lisa?" Having this question on my final exam, so to speak, helps me decide how good of a grade I want from God in response to serving my wife, Lisa.

Lisa actually knows much of what I am going to share with you in the following pages. She is a servant to me, our children, and those in our office. She taught me this by example. For more than twenty-nine years, Lisa and Jesus have poured a lot into me about becoming a servant.

I want to expose you to the heart of serving. Hopefully, as you see this, you will hear and reflect on these words on a daily basis, "Well done good and faithful servant." This relates to the amazing servant you have been toward your spouse.

Called

When you hear a young man or woman say, "I'm called," what images come to your mind? Probably several. You might think of the person who goes down to the altar of your church and feels at a very deep level that they are "called" to be a missionary, preacher, or teacher."

When they "receive the call," everything changes. The way they look at themselves is totally different than moments before receiving the call. They suddenly have a purpose for their lives and a sense of knowing why their Creator has made them. They also seem to have a passion for their newfound calling. I do not mean just an emotional temporary high, but a strong multidecade passion for their area of ministry.

One other thing that happens to this called soul is he or she begins to define himself or herself by the calling: "I'm going to be . . ." or "I am . . . a pastor/teacher/_____."
This calling is much more than their present 9 to 5 job. It is an expression of who they are, almost at a DNA level. This person becomes their calling.

We all know someone who is so passionate about something that it really becomes who they are. Their passion is what we think about when we characterize the person in our minds.

Lastly, a called person seems to innately accept a season of education or training for this calling he or she received. They might go to Bible school, seminary, or an intern program in order to discipline their lives to be effective on a sustainable basis for their calling.

Thankfully, the church by now has accepted that every believer has a calling, whether it be office manager, politician, or grocery clerk. All are called and all are in full-time ministry all the time.

Just as we have a calling to a vocation and/or ministry, many of us have a calling to marriage. If marriage is part of your calling, it is important to understand it if you intend to grow in it. Without understanding the call to be married, you will look at marriage mostly through secular lenses and focus your evaluation of the marriage on how happy you are, and not on how well you are serving your spouse.

Here is just a little bit more about calling. When you answer your cell phone, it has a cool feature on it that tells you who is calling (if you have them in your contacts list). It is important to know who is calling you. When anyone is called to a vocation, ministry, or marriage (and so on), who does the calling? God.

God, the Almighty, the awesome, all-knowing, all-present, all-powerful Creator is the one who calls you into salvation, ministry, vocation, and yes—He alone has called you into marriage. He alone is the one to whom you will answer for the quality of service toward your spouse. He alone will move you into various stages of preparation and progress as you pass through the various adventures of marriage.

It is God who has called me to serve Lisa. She alone is my first ministry—above my children (as wonderful as they are), any public ministry or vocation or responsibility, my house responsibilities, workouts, hobbies, or adventures. The only calling above ministry to Lisa is my ministry to love and serve my Lord and Savior Jesus Christ.

Now I will be up front; I am not perfect. However, anyone who knows me knows I am committed. During my education, parenting, or working I made no excuses not to date Lisa, assist around the house, or to help the kids with homework, because this is my calling. Every cell in my body accepts that I am called to be a servant to Lisa.

Accepting my role as a servant (and the ongoing revelations of what that means) has so far been a twenty-nine year journey of growth, repentance, and expansion of my servant heart toward Lisa. I started off young, immature, selfish, impatient, and unkind—like many married people do. Today, I accept my role as a servant. I am called to serve, period.

I recall a favorite funny story about being a servant. One day, when we were in the middle of two kids in school, working a full private counseling practice, writing books, and speaking at conferences, I had a moment. You know, one of those moments when God uses everyday life events to expose our less-than-wonderful human heart?

It was late in the week, about 3:45 p.m., and I was driving home after a busy day at my counseling office. Lisa had just picked up the children from school and was already home.

That's when it happened.

I got a call from Lisa, saying, "Hey, can you pick up _____ (such and such) on the way home?" At that time, my usual practice was to do such things, though begrudgingly. However, this time, I was somehow offended or insulted that she had even asked. I am sure I was short on the phone, though I did stop and pick it up.

When I got home, I expected a hero's welcome because I had picked up whatever it was. However, Lisa, remembering my shortness on the phone, was not that happy to see me, and there was some tension between us for a few minutes.

I remember God revealing something to me right then. I began looking at a system of behaviors that led to consistent results: I get a 3:45 p.m. call; I act short; I do the errand anyway; I get no credit for doing it because of my attitude; we have tension in our marriage, and; I am 100 percent responsible for this cycle every time it occurs. Since I help marriages for a living, this insight led me to do what I call, "Take Responsibility and Solve the Problem" (very clinical).

How can I change this pattern? I wondered. I cannot stop the call because that is just part of real life with a real family—plus, she is just asking for legitimate help. I came up with the thought of just answering the phone differently. After thinking about that a while, I do believe the Holy Spirit (so thankful for Him) whispered my new response to Lisa: "This is your servant. How can I help you?"

I was ready the next time a 3:45 p.m. call came in. When Lisa called, I literally answered: "This is your servant. How can I help you?" First, this put my heart exactly where it needed to be at the time. I was not "Dr. Weiss," I was Lisa's servant. Second, doing whatever needed to be done was not so distasteful to me. When I got home, I got a much better welcome, and was met with closeness and warmth instead of tension and coldness. All of this was the result of me accepting my true calling and role.

Afterward, a funny thing happened one day when I picked up the children and a few of their friends from school when Lisa called. For the first time, our children and their friends heard me answer the phone: "This is your servant. How can I help you?" They thought it was hilarious and got a big laugh out of it. Over the years, they got it: Marriage is not only about serving; it is about serving well with a good attitude.

You and I are absolutely called to be married. This calling comes from God. Our quality and attitude will be assessed by God Himself. We are not called to be served; we are called to serve.

I am aware that I am going to move some of you from a fundamentally worldly perspective of marriage into a kingdom type paradigm of marriage. However, when you have wrong beliefs and follow through with them, you get wrong results. It is essential to learn and internalize right beliefs.

I work a lot with people with addictions. These people have bought into a set of beliefs that are incredibly destructive to themselves and those around them, yet they continue them as long as they can. Only when they change their beliefs will their lives change and their addiction be broken. Similarly, as you change your beliefs and behaviors in marriage and accept new life-giving paradigms and truths, you will follow through, have amazing results, and live a very productive and godly life.

There is another important truth about addicts that also applies to those whose destructive thoughts have hurt or weakened their marriage. Some addicts undergo a grief process before they are able to accept that they were addicted and fully responsible before their lives can heal and change. Why is this important? Unless they accept that they are addicts, they remain in a battle with their painful reality because it continually revisits them, and they are less able to take responsibility.

It can be challenging to truly accept in your heart that you are a servant in your marriage. You may have pre-conceived notions based on your culture, your parent's marriage, something you thought was "biblical," or things you just flat-out made up to make marriage work better for you.

I had all of these thoughts, just as you may well have. It has taken over two decades for the Lord to highlight, expose, and sometimes beat out of me a bad idea or paradigm I truly believed in my heart about marriage, and my servant role and calling. So, I want you to know the grief process right up front because some of the kingdom principles I will expose you to in this book can be downright painful to let go of as they are so attached to your heart and current secular lifestyle.

It is important you know about grief so you will know what is happening if you feel it as you read this book. Grieving is good. It means you are in the process of trying to accept a new reality—a kingdom marriage reality that I like to call the servant marriage.

"We are not called to be served; we are called to serve."

Making the First Servant Marriage

These next few chapters are going to be an amazing journey into the heart of God as He creates His master-piece—marriage. Marriage is by far the most complex of all God's creations. In this chapter, I want to take you on a three-phase journey through His creation of this amaz-ing masterpiece. I do so by comparing it to a house; something with which you can probably relate.

Way before a house is ever successfully built, several be-hind the scenes activities must occur. First, consideration is given to the environment, the land. Does the parcel work? Can it support a house? Is the size adequate? Does water run off it properly? Which is the best posi-tion for the house, given the direction from which the sun rises? Where should the driveway go? The environ-ment has a lot to do with how the house is designed and built.

Next, the design of the whole house is created. Behind every house is a man or woman who takes all the envi-ronmental issues into consideration, and applies all his or her engineering genius and creativity to draw up plans for the house.

Finally, the builder gets involved. This is basically a three-phase process:

> • Phase one concerns the foundation, including plumbing and electrical considerations.
> • Phase two concerns the process of creating the structure. This includes the walls, the roof, electricity, plumbing, air conditioning, heat, and more.
> • Phase three is the finale. The builder applies paint, lays carpet, and adds finishing touches to the house to bring to life what the engineers imagined.

A marriage is quite a creation indeed and a marriage has an all-knowing, all-powerful Creator who designed the environment even before he started to create his masterpiece. However, like any great designer or engineer, He started with the end creation of marriage in mind the entire time. He started with the environment in which the marriage would live.

I will lead you on a quick jaunt through this amazing environment our God created for marriage to enjoy.

[1]In the beginning God created the heavens and the earth. [2] Now the earth was formless and empty, darkness was over the surface of the deep, and the Spirit of God was hovering over the waters.

³ And God said, "Let there be light," and there was light. ⁴ God saw that the light was good, and he separated the light from the darkness. ⁵ God called the light "day," and the darkness he called "night." And there was evening, and there was morning—the first day.

⁶ And God said, "Let there be a vault between the waters to separate water from water."⁷ So God made the vault and separated the water under the vault from the water above it. And it was so. ⁸ God called the vault "sky." And there was evening, and there was morning—the second day.

⁹ And God said, "Let the water under the sky be gathered to one place, and let dry ground appear." And it was so. ¹⁰ God called the dry ground "land," and the gathered water she called "seas." And God saw that it was good.

¹¹ Then God said, "Let the land produce vegetation: seed-bearing plants and trees on the land that bear fruit with seed in it, according to their various kinds." And it was so.¹² The land produced vegetation: plants bearing seed according to their kinds and trees bearing fruit with seed in it according to their kinds. And God saw that it was good. ¹³ And there was evening, and there was morning—the third day.

¹⁴ And God said, "Let there be lights in the vault of the sky to separate the day from the night, and let them serve as signs to mark sacred times, and days and years, ¹⁵ and let them be lights in the vault of the sky to give light on the earth." And it was so.¹⁶ God made two great lights— the greater light to govern the day and the lesser light to govern the night. He also made the stars. ¹⁷ God set them in the vault of the sky to give light on the earth, ¹⁸ to govern the day and the night, and to separate light from darkness. And God saw that it was good. ¹⁹ And there was

evening, and there was morning—the fourth day.
²⁰ And God said, "Let the water teem with living crea-
tures, and let birds fly above the earth across the vault
of the sky." ²¹ So God created the great creatures of the
sea and every living thing with which the water teems
and that moves about in it, according to their kinds, and
every winged bird according to its kind. And God saw that
it was good. ²² God blessed them and said, "Be fruitful and
increase in number and fill the water in the seas, and let
the birds increase on the earth." ²³ And there was evening,
and there was morning—the fifth day.
²⁴ And God said, "Let the land produce living creatures ac-
cording to their kinds: the livestock, the creatures that
move along the ground, and the wild animals, each ac-
cording to its kind." And it was so. ²⁵ God made the wild
animals according to their kinds, the livestock according
to their kinds, and all the creatures that move along the
ground according to their kinds. And God saw that it was
good.
Genesis 1:1-25, NIV

This is the environment in which God would then create
His masterpiece. He created the heavens so we could
see the stars, feel the breeze, enjoy the seasons, and eat
awesome food. This is the Master Builder's first phase of
His masterpiece called marriage.

Genesis 2:4-25 (NIV) describes stage two of God's plan in
creating marriage.

⁴ This is the account of the heavens and the earth when
they were created, when the LORD God made the earth
and the heavens.

⁵ Now no shrub had yet appeared on the earth[a] and no plant had yet sprung up, for theLORD God had not sent rain on the earth and there was no one to work the ground, ⁶ but streams[b] came up from the earth and watered the whole surface of the ground. ⁷ Then the LORD God formed a man[c] from the dust of the ground and breathed into his nostrils the breath of life, and the man became a living being.

⁸ Now the LORD God had planted a garden in the east, in Eden; and there he put the man he had formed. ⁹ The LORD God made all kinds of trees grow out of the ground—trees that were pleasing to the eye and good for food. In the middle of the garden were the tree of life and the tree of the knowledge of good and evil.

¹⁰ A river watering the garden flowed from Eden; from there it was separated into four headwaters. ¹¹ The name of the first is the Pishon; it winds through the entire land of Havilah, where there is gold. ¹² (The gold of that land is good; aromatic resin[d] and onyx are also there.) ¹³ The name of the second river is the Gihon; it winds through the entire land of Cush. ¹⁴ The name of the third river is the Tigris; it runs along the east side of Ashur. And the fourth river is the Euphrates.

¹⁵ The LORD God took the man and put him in the Garden of Eden to work it and take care of it. ¹⁶ And the LORD God commanded the man, "You are free to eat from any tree in the garden; ¹⁷ but you must not eat from the tree of the knowledge of good and evil, for when you eat from it you will certainly die."

¹⁸ The LORD God said, "It is not good for the man to be alone. I will make a helper suitable for him."

¹⁹ Now the LORD God had formed out of the ground all the wild animals and all the birds in the sky. He brought

them to the man to see what he would name them; and whatever the man called each living creature, that was its name. ²⁰ So the man gave names to all the livestock, the birds in the sky and all the wild animals.

But for Adam no suitable helper was found. ²¹ So the LORD God caused the man to fall into a deep sleep; and while he was sleeping, he took one of the man's ribs and then closed up the place with flesh. ²² Then the LORD God made a woman from the rib he had taken out of the man, and he brought her to the man.

²³ The man said,

> *"This is now bone of my bones*
> *and flesh of my flesh;*
> *she shall be called 'woman,'*
> *for she was taken out of man."*

²⁴ That is why a man leaves his father and mother and is united to his wife, and they become one flesh.

²⁵ Adam and his wife were both naked, and they felt no shame.

One important observation about the making of man is found in verse 5; "and there was no man to work the ground." The purpose of man existed before he was created. Man was created to be a solution on earth. His purpose was established *before* his creation.

Jeremiah 1:5 (NIV) also speaks to this idea that our purpose was created before our creation: "Before I formed you in the womb, I knew you, before you were born I set you apart; I appointed you as a prophet to the nations."

Adam's purpose was to work the ground. I believe every person made by God believes he or she has a purpose. As he or she seeks God, in time (sometimes over decades), the plan and purposes are revealed and manifested. Each of us are here to solve a problem. When we find out what it is and are willing to accept responsibility for it, we can release the solution on any scale God allows.

So, Adam had his great hair, muscles, skin, eyes, brain, heart, and all the magnificence of being a creature. Had God stopped here, Adam would have just been an animal with opposing thumb features as an upgrade.

Then, the amazing miracle that has separated Adam from all creatures big and small occurred. God "breathed into his nostrils the breath of life, and the man became a living creature" (Genesis 2:7, NIV). God graciously breathed into Adam the very breath of life. He breathed Himself into us. We have the divine spark, if you will, that no other animal on the planet has. Then God placed him in the Garden, "to work" (Genesis 2:15).

I tell my single lady friends that this is the order of God. First, God gives a man a job, then later a spouse. I will get to why in a moment, but this is very important in understanding the heart of a man.

Men were created for the purpose of work. Their task orientation is God-given. It is critical that women understand this about men.

As I write this, I am sitting in a Kentucky airport on a Saturday after doing a marriage conference. I just called Lisa to check in on her to see how she is doing. Then she asked me what I was doing, since I had some time before my flight back to Colorado Springs.

"I'm writing," I responded.

"Why don't you take it easy?" she asked.

"That's not what I do," I said.

I get pleasure from writing book after book. I see these books impact lives, so it gives me pleasure to "push a pen" for hours at a time to make that possible. Men are created to work.

Interestingly, the next thing God gives Adam is a boundary. "And the Lord commanded the man, 'You are free to eat from any tree in the garden, but you must not eat from the tree of the knowledge of good and evil, for when you eat of it, you will certainly die'" (Genesis 2:16-17, NIV).

I find it interesting that immediately after giving Adam a job, God gives him a boundary with a predetermined consequence. This is actually good parenting; to set boundaries with clear consequences for your child.

God then moves to stage two of His masterpiece called marriage. This stage is a very powerful one, and it is imperative for us to understand it if we are to actualize a servant marriage.

In my thirty plus years of being a Christian, I have never heard a sermon on what I am about to share with you. This is something that downloaded to me while I was sitting in another airport in Canada and reading the scripture below for roughly the thousandth time. I have preached this scripture hundreds of times (easily) and yet I never saw something in it so significant that it radically changed my perspective of God's final creation—marriage—forever. It changed it so much that I had to write a whole book about it so we could all have incredible servant marriages.

"The Lord God said, 'It is not good for the man to be alone. I will make a helper suitable for him'" (Genesis 2:18, NIV). Notice that women and marriage were both God's ideas. Man did not create women or marriage; only God can do that.

Go quickly back over God's creation account in Genesis chapters 1 and 2 and you will see it is all relatively similar: God speaks, it exists; God speaks, He makes it exist. This is not so with women or marriage.

In verse 18, God says He will create a helper for Adam. However, He did not get around to actually doing it until verse 21. Why the break in pattern? Why did God not just speak Eve into existence instantly, or speak and make her right there and then? Adam's aloneness did not change between verses 18 and 21.

The reason is this: God had to prepare Adam for his final creation—marriage. Though Adam was alone, he was unskilled and unprepared to be the kind of servant he would need to be in a marriage.

Up to that point, Adam had enjoyed the "single life," so to speak. He ate when he wanted to, hung out with the chimps or lions at night, had a good time, and only had to think of himself. Adam had to become a servant *before* God could trust him with His final creation of a woman and marriage.

Adam had to undergo a miraculous process of becoming a servant before he would be able to receive a woman and a marriage. Through this process, God chose to continue to create Adam. <u>Before</u> He would create His masterpiece, God's goal was to create a servant-hearted man in the Garden—not simply to create a man. It would be a lot harder to create servant marriage without first creating the foundational element—a servant. God gave Adam a heart, but He still needed to create a servant-hearted man.

In Genesis 2:19-20 (NIV) we read: "Now the Lord God had formed out of the ground all the beauty of the field and all the birds of the air. He brought them to the man to see what he would name them: and whatever the man called each living creature, that was its name. So, the man gave names to all the livestock, the birds of the air and all the beasts of the field."

Walk with me in your mind a little bit and picture what was actually happening in Adam's life. God was moving him from just meeting his needs to meet the needs of others. Adam was not in the Garden for himself. He was created to serve—to serve others. Though Adam had a mature body, he was not as mature as the Father who lived a servant lifestyle in heaven with the Son and Holy Spirit. So, just as any father starts his child out with simple and then increasingly complex tasks as the child develops, the Father began creating the DNA of a servant in Adam the only way it can be created; by serving.

So, after a good night's sleep, Adam got up early (this is my guess, because I think God is an early riser). He saw God off in the distance, collecting a herd of unique animals that moved at varying speeds. Looking like a shepherd of a particularly unique herd of various animals, God sauntered to the place where Adam was shepherding and brought the animals to that place. Then he pulled up a rock or something else to sit on as all day long as Adam looked at each animal and gave it a name. There is quite a bit right here about creating a servant.

Finally, with God showing up every day, Adam had to get used to some form of regimen. This is important because the climactic event for which God was preparing Adam—marriage—is a daily sport. For this, Adam had to engage one of his greatest gifts: creativity. I am sure God and Adam had some genuine moments of laughter, smiling, and even blank stares as Adam spoke: "Aardvark, zebra, giraffe," and so on.

Take a moment and consider how many different types of birds, livestock, and mammals existed then. We know many have gone extinct for one reason or another, so when you think of them, imagine even more animals. (You might be able to Google lists of the many birds and animals that are known to exist.) Even if all you had to do was read such a list, it would take you a pretty long time. Now, imagine how long it would take for every one of those animals to walk up to you, be evaluated by you (maybe have them do something or demonstrate a unique talent to help inspire you), and then from scratch—with no previous reference point and never having read anything—for you to create a name for each animal.

How long do you think it took Adam to complete this task? Weeks? Months? Years? I have no idea, but I do know it was not immediate. God was creating a servant man; a man who was not here for himself, but to serve others.

Adam had to accept responsibility for the needs of the animals all day long. People also have needs all day long, whether at work or home. It was vitally important for Adam to see the needs of others as opportunities to serve; not as impositions or inconveniences that would keep him from doing what he thought he might be entitled to do at any given moment.

These needs were brought to Adam every day, day after day, for a very long time. Serving was not just what Adam did, it was becoming who he was.

Adam's daily acceptance of this responsibility was important. The need of the animals to be named was a real, legitimate need. In marriage, you and I are face-to-face with real, legitimate needs on a regular basis.

What was the need Adam was meeting every day as God sat and watched him work every day; day in and day out? It was the legitimate need for identity.

The animals were created by God; they were given identity by man. Each animal had a God-given ache in its heart to have a name and identity. I am sure God had no problem getting a herd together after the first day.

I can only imagine not knowing how or if animals could communicate, but somehow being able to understand Adam's communication. For example, let's say a squirrel and a pigeon were in the first herd to approach Adam. Imagine a squirrel standing in front of Adam, sitting up, clearly prepared to receive his name. Then imagine Adam looking at the little animal, pausing, smiling, and then saying, "squirrel."

"Squirrel," you can almost hear the squirrel saying. "I'm squirrel."

"I am squirrel," he might have repeated so often that it eventually frustrated the unnamed animals. "Who are you?" he would then ask a given animal.

"I don't know," the unnamed animal would reply. "I have yet to meet the man, Adam."

The pigeon did the same thing; approaching unnamed animals and saying, "I am pigeon, who are you?"

The response was the same: "I don't know. I have yet to meet the man, Adam." Day after day, the birds also began to groan, they so desired to be named by the man.

You see, the need for identity of all creation was being met by the man, Adam, and his voice. All day long, Adam spoke and creatures rejoiced. Sound familiar? Speaking to create, Adam was becoming a servant like his Father.

His Father (God), specifically the Lord God, would leave heaven, come down, gather some eager animals, grab a seat, hang out, laugh, and enjoy watching His son become like Him; a servant.

Through a process, God was imparting to Adam the ability to be responsible with the needs and identities of those around him. This was training to prepare Adam for the final stages of God's creation; a woman, and then marriage.

This servant process is so critical. Had Adam not become a servant prior to marriage, he would have been totally ill-equipped to handle the needs of a woman, the needs of marriage, and the needs of a family. This foundational training is what God knows we need to be successful in marriage.

If we come at our marriage to be served instead of to serve the other person, we are setting ourselves up for significant, unnecessary pain. If a man or woman is not a servant, he or she is not ready for marriage. If there is not a servant at the very core of who you are, you have totally missed why you are here on planet Earth, and why you are married and received a family. Each responsibility is designed to expand your ability and capacity to serve with excellence and a great attitude.

The servant DNA in Adam became the second stage of God's creation of marriage. Just as Adam was created from dirt, Eve would be created from the bone and blood of a servant man.

In his process of becoming a servant, Adam learned several key things. He learned to be responsible for others. He learned to be consistent. He learned to be creative on a daily basis. He learned to work hard, obey God, and enjoy God's presence during work.

Adam learned how to do his part. God did what was amazing and miraculous by creating the animals, then bringing them to Adam. Then, as part of learning how to be on a team, Adam did his part. Marriage is a lot like this. God does His miraculous part and we do our part—serving.

God was now ready to move toward the next stage of His creation of marriage by creating woman.

"But for Adam no suitable helper was found. So the Lord God caused the man to fall into a deep sleep; and while he was sleeping, he took one of the man's ribs and closed up the place with flesh. Then the Lord God made a woman from the rib he had taken out of the man" (Genesis 2:21-22, NIV).

This is an amazing event. God took time to train and create a serving man. In this time, I am sure He watched what made Adam smile, laugh, get exasperated, and more. He could truly see what and who Adam needed. I am so glad He had Adam sleep during this process. God did not need Adam's thoughts or opinions about who or what woman would be. Adam had no ability to design a creature that would carry children and have several unique features women have. God was on the scene doing what He does—creating.

God created Eve. Why did Eve not need all the training Adam required? Adam was the foundation of this building called marriage. He was created from dirt as a man and became a servant.

Eve was created with DNA from a servant. She was given servant DNA from the beginning. This answered a lifelong question for me: Why is it that women in every culture seem to innately and intuitively get the ideas of selflessness, consideration for others, and being creative and consistent in serving? They get it from Adam's servant DNA. They originated from much greater DNA than mere dirt. My wife, Lisa, and many women do not struggle as much as men do with the lower nature. It is as if they get this DNA thing at—dare I say—a cellular level.

The scripture says that "he brought her to the man" (Genesis 2:22, NIV). This is important. God walked with Eve for a while before He brought her to Adam. Eve and God had their own relationship. This is important as God moves toward His final creation in the Garden—

marriage. I cannot wait to watch the heavenly DVD that will show us what God and Eve talked about, and how long their trip was. Regardless of the details, God first established Himself in Eve's heart before He introduced her to Adam.

Take a moment to think about what it took for you to marry your spouse. You can plainly see that your marriage is a miracle—a supernatural act of the Lord God Almighty on your behalf.

First, God had to put you both in the same time zone of human history. Then He had to get you to meet by moving one of you across town, state, or even across the nations to meet. Then He confused one of you (just kidding) and then you got married.

Seriously though, almost every marriage I have worked with—saved or not—has its own stories of supernatural things that occurred and cemented or verified to both spouses that the other person was the one each should marry.

I do want to make a quick, important point. When God took the rib from Adam, He "closed up the place with flesh" (Genesis 2:21, NIV). God healed Adam from this wound before He brought the woman to him. God did not want this marriage He was about to create to be based upon Adam's woundedness. God also did not want Adam to looked to Eve as a source of healing. Only God can heal us; not a spouse.

I have been abandoned, sexually abused, addicted, and more. I had to take responsibility to heal those wounds. Do not let your marriage foundation be your wounds, but rather let the foundation be God healing those wounds. If you need professional help here, I suggest you get it to heal the wounds and inherit a better you in a marriage.

The scene for God's final creation was set. He made Adam a man, then a servant, and then He made Eve with servant DNA. Then God did something very familiar to Adam, but quite different this day.

It was normal for Adam to wake from sleep and see God walking toward him with a herd. That day, he saw God walking toward him, but there was no herd making its noisy way up to Adam's house that time. That day, one amazingly beautiful creature walked with God toward Adam.

As she walked up, I am sure Adam was wowed. I am sure excitement, wonder, and all kinds of feelings and hormones went off inside Adam's mind and body.

However, he had been trained by God. He knew his place was to serve and think about her needs—her need for identity, her need to be spoken to. Adam was ready to participate in the final creation of God: marriage.

Adam said, "This is now bone of my bones and flesh of my flesh; she shall be called 'woman,' for she was taken out of man" (Genesis 2:23, NIV).

As his first step into marriage, Adam served. He met Eve's need. He gave her identity. When he did, I am sure every creature in sight roared, squealed, or otherwise applauded this first marriage. This was the final creation of God on earth.

God was creating a trinity on earth, just as it is in heaven. He created Adam and made him a servant because only servant DNA could actualize the triune lifestyle. Then He created a trinity, a servant trinity on earth, just as it is in heaven. Three beings all loving one another and serving and sacrificing for the others. This was what God wanted for mankind: He wanted them to become one. This unity would be the environment into which the human race could have been born, had sin not entered the picture.

But thanks be to God who became a man in Christ Jesus and died for our sins so we could once again experience this trinity on earth called marriage—the *servant marriage*!

"Do not let your marriage foundation be your wounds, but rather let the foundation be God healing those wounds."

Father-in-Law

In the last chapter, we explored the beauty of God making a trinity on earth as it is in heaven. God was making a three-faced servant being on earth to multiply trinities, raise children, and glorify His name.

This trinity idea is no minor thought on marriage. Marriage being a trinity between God, man, and woman is what separates a Christian definition of marriage from every version or perversion of marriage any culture or individual can decide upon.

Do you remember a while back when the media in America tried to use marriage to create one of its fads, asking whether marriage was only between a man and a woman? Even some of the best and brightest in Christianity were duped into answering a question that, even in its formation, limited the Christian definition of marriage.

From a Christian perspective, marriage is not and never has been between a man and a woman. A Christian marriage, as shown in Genesis 1 and 2, is between God, a man, and a woman.

When a culture or individuals remove God from marriage, anything can occur. After all, in some cultures beating one's wife is a normal practice. Even Christians in such cultures might spank their wives when they feel they need to be spanked because they have a secular understanding of marriage. Regardless of cultural belief, when you or I believe that marriage is just between a man and a woman, the fruit of this secular idea will show up in our marriage.

I have seen so many Christians shipwreck their lives and their marriages due to this secular view of marriage—that it is just between the two of them. Well, in our secular culture, there is also an idea that marriage is supposed to make one happy. So, if your spouse is not making you happy, this is a justifiable reason for you to Facebook old lovers, cheat on your spouse, or divorce them.

One woman I counseled served in a leadership role in her church. She separated from her husband and had a series of one night stands because he was not having enough sex with her. When I told her she was still married to Jesus and not just to her husband, and that she had no biblical right to be sexual outside of marriage, she became indignant and angry with me. Even she, a Christian leader, had a secular view of marriage.

Many men attempt to use Scripture to dominate women because, "The Man is the Head." They fail to recognize that Scripture actually calls them to be a servant head just like Christ is to the church; a servant who answers to God.

I have seen men with hierarchical cultural views try to Christianize this secular idea. They use their supposed authority over their God-given wives to beat, emotionally abuse, rape, and financially control them. When a secular, godless view of marriage is created, there is no limit to the human ability to justify abusive behavior in the marriage as "just between my spouse and I."

I have known of Christian couples that had open marriages in which either spouse could cheat whenever they wanted because the two of them "agreed" on this. This is crazy, but they started with a secular idea: Marriage is just us two and we make the rules.

Newsflash: Marriage is not just between a man and a woman; it is between God, a man, and a woman, and He makes the rules, not the humans in the marriage.

You can tell I could go on and on about the damage a secular idea of marriage can have among Christians. I have heard of lust, pornography, online affairs, actual affairs, prostitution, lying, secret accounts or phones or credit cards, and more. These Christians engage in this behavior as if God does not exist, does not know, and will not address these issues in a marriage to his child. The wood floors in my office are stained with tears every week because of Christians who believe their marriage was just between the two of them, and that God was not the third person in their marriage.

In this trinity of marriage, we humans are equal in value. One does not rule over the other. A man is not a king in the triune marriage—God is. If a man thinks he can be king over an all-knowing, all-powerful God, he may be suffering from a delusion of grandeur.

I know God is the King of my marriage to Lisa. We both seek Him to guide us to serve each other and make wise decisions. God is a very known person in our marriage, and I pray He is in your servant marriage as well.

If for any reason you have not believed God is the third real person in your marriage, I want you to thoughtfully read this chapter and reflect on these ideas. In my understanding, God created my marriage and I am a participant in what He is doing on planet Earth, including my marriage.

God was never meant to be an afterthought in a Christian marriage. His role was never meant to be seasonal or accidental. He was never meant to merely be our 9-1-1 guy when we need help. He is to intentionally be the first person to whom we both relate, individually and together, on a very regular basis.

Two Relationships

I think we established that God is a real caring person in our marriages. Have you ever thought about how God feels as a member of your marriage? Do you think God feels wanted, pursued, loved, honored, considered, and engaged in your marriage? Or do you think God feels unwanted, disrespected, and silenced in your marriage? God does have feelings. How does he feel in your marriage? Answering this question as a couple can really open your eyes to the amazing first person in your marriage.

I want to talk to you about the two relationships you both have with God in your marriage. I will start with the one with which it is likely you are most familiar: God as your Father.

In Western culture especially, we emphasize our personal relationship with Christ. This is a good thing for us to see and relate to God as our Father or Abba. He cares for us deeply as individuals. He wants only the best for us and has good gifts for us. He is a Father, so He is totally okay with us growing up and going through stages of life, and He is willing to guide or correct us as we walk this journey called life together.

Whether our earthly dad was less than perfect or wonderful, we can transcend that experience and experience God as a dad who cares. I love having an all-knowing, all-powerful God as my dad. In my life, He and I have faced many things, and I love learning about Him in my day-to-day life.

Then there comes a second relationship you have with God when you are in a triune marriage. This relationship is not with God as Father, but rather, with God as your **Father-in-law**. God is the one who created, birthed, and matured your spouse—the same God who brought he or she into your life to be your spouse. Your spouse is God's favorite son or daughter, so this makes you a son-in-law to His favored daughter or a daughter-in-law to His favored son.

You are not just a son or daughter of God. You are a son-in-law or daughter of God. You are a daughter-in-law or son of God as well. When you marry, you have two relationships with God; one as a son or daughter and one as a son-in-law or daughter-in-law.

For just a minute, think about this concept of being an in-law of God. Remember how I asked you to imagine how God feels in your marriage? Now I want you to imagine how God feels toward you as an in-law.

Does God feel proud of you? Is He encouraged—even thankful—that He gave your spouse to you to love? Alternatively, does God feel regret, sadness, or even dislike over how you have treated the person you call your spouse?

I realize many of you have never ever thought about God—the all-knowing, ever-present, all-powerful God—as your actual Father-in-law. He sees all the thoughts and behaviors you have toward your spouse, whether you are with them or absent from them.

Expectations

Some of you reading this have already reached where you are the father-in-law or mother-in-law of your child.

Regardless of the current ages of your children, most of you will one day be an in-law to your children's spouse. When you are an in-law, this is a totally different relationship than being a father or mother of a child. You are 100 percent trusting that man or woman will be responsible to genuinely love, honor, and cherish your child. You cannot control or really influence what that person does, but how they love your child does impact you.

Actually, I think how they love your child will be the largest factor by far as to how you feel toward that in-law. Their love or lack of love for your child is a primary factor in your relationship with them.

This expectation that you will love, honor, and cherish your spouse is no different with God. God as a Father-in-law expects you to love your spouse. He expects you to learn the way to love them and serve them, demonstrating His love and your love to them on a consistent, though imperfect basis.

Have you ever thought of what God the Father-in-Law's expectations are for you in your marriage? When you take a moment to think about this, how do you think you are doing in regard to His expectations of you as a son-in-law or daughter-in-law?

I have known God as my Father-in-Law for many years. He is kind. He gives me revelation and wisdom to love and serve Lisa. He constantly reminds me of her value to Him. Honestly, I think He smiles upon me when I am getting this loving and serving thing right toward Lisa.

Empowerment

Unlike our earthly in-laws, our Father-in-Law, God, has unlimited resources for us to carry out His expectations of excellence in serving and loving our spouses. Think through with me of all He has given to you to enable you to be an excellent, loving servant to your spouse.

First, He gave you the death of His Son so you could break strongholds of sin in your life in order to serve with excellence. He has given you the gift of the Holy Spirit to live inside you to help you be an excellent son-in-law or daughter-in-law. He has given you the Word of God, the Bible, to help you grow daily in the wisdom of how to love.

He has given you a community of faith in the local church. There you see love being worked out in people's lives. He has given you finances, time, and a heart touched by His grace and love so you can be an excellent son-in-law or daughter-in-law.

God has done quite a bit for me to enable me to be successful as a loving servant toward my spouse. I will never be able to say He did not give me all I needed to love and serve my wife well.

How about you? Has the Father lavished resources and opportunities on you to love and serve your spouse with excellence? The answer is yes for all of us who call Jesus Lord. How we utilize these amazing resources of God is up to us, but I do not think any of us can argue that He has not amply supplied resources for us to be in-laws of God.

Another resource I love and encourage couples to use is prayer. By this I do not mean your daily couples prayer, though it is a great idea to have that in your life. It is true that this practice can only lead to God having good feelings toward you as you bring your spouse to Him every day in joint prayer. I am talking instead of praying directly to God, the Father-in-Law.

I provide below both male and female examples of what this prayer might sound like at critical times when you reconnect after one or both finish working for the day.

John praying as he pulls into the driveway or garage of his house:

Father-in-Law God, I am about to enter the zone here at my house. My wife has served endlessly today and is probably quite spent. Give me wisdom to see what needs to be done with the children, the house, or just her heart. Father-in-Law God, give me the energy for the first hour or so to serve well with a great attitude and put my needs last for at least an hour or so. Please hear your son-in-law's prayer. I love you, Jesus.

Jane's prayer for the Father-in-Law God as she sees John pulling up to the house:

Father-in-Law God, thank you for a great husband who worked hard today to provide for our family, as this is one of the ways he loves the children and me. Let my kiss remind him he has a lover, not just a wife. Give me wisdom to know how to encourage him and thank him tonight for what he does around here. I love you, Father, and I thank you for the opportunity to show and speak love to your son today.

Imagine if you prayed like this every day for a week, month, or years. You would start getting the Father's heart for your spouse. You would be more grateful and energized in your marriage—at least that is how it affects me. When I pray to Father-in-Law God, acknowledging Lisa as His gift to me, it changes my attitude and energy as I enter my marriage and family. With that energy I feel less self-centered and entitled to get my needs met above all, and almost naturally move toward serving without having a negative attitude about it.

Try the Father-in-Law prayer for a while. Each time you pray, check it off on a sticky note or on your phone to validate your consistency. See what this simple prayer can do for you and your marriage.

Accountability

You know that day you got married was a special occasion. Go back to that moment when the groom/soon-to-be husband stood by the pastor with the groomsmen. Just then, the silence is broken when those famous notes of the wedding march, "Here Comes the Bride," ring out. As the song plays, the stunning creation called a bride starts walking down the aisle. Everyone is focused on the stunning beauty.

Now go back to that memory and widen your frame a little bit more. Do you see that man standing next to and actually walking down the aisle with that beautiful creature called a bride? Oh yes, there he is—the groom's future father-in-law.

Even in the wedding ceremony, there is a hint that the groom has some accountability to the man who walks his daughter down the aisle. Likewise, as Christians, we have accountability to the Father-in-Law God for our behavior and attitude toward our spouses.

There is a saying in business success literature that goes something like this: "Start with the end in mind." Take that to the very end—your final breath on earth. You are standing before the Lord to give an account for your entire life spent here on earth. As you face your Father-in-Law, how would you like that conversation to go?

> A. "Well done, good and faithful servant, you have loved and served your spouse amazingly."
>
> B. "Well, you were really average—at best—in the way you loved the spouse I gave you as a gift."
>
> C. "You were really awful at loving my child, your spouse. It was all about you and I am sad you did not learn to serve well on earth."

I do not know about you, but I would rather have conversation "A" rather than "B" or "C."

This reminds me of a conversation I had with a student who had very low grades in his first semester of college. When I asked what his strategy was to improve the issue, he said: "This semester, I am aiming for a 4.0. That way, if I get a lower grade, I will still do well."

This is what I always like about life. There is always a next chapter or next season in life. Regardless at how well or not so well we have loved and served our spouse, we get another season.

It is playoff season for football as I write this chapter. It strikes me that no team starts the season strategizing about the team they will play in the Super Bowl. Everyone knows you have to play each game well to get to the playoffs, and so on.

In the recovery community, they have a saying that goes like this: "One day at a time." This simply means the alcoholics are not thinking about getting a twenty year chip for sobriety, but on doing what it takes to stay sober today.

Understanding there is an end is important. How you play the sport of marriage on a daily basis is the process to get you to hear, "Well done, good and faithful servant." When I accept that I am accountable to the Father-in-Law God daily for how I treat my spouse and the attitudes I express toward her (spoken or not), I serve and love better. Being accountable to my Father-in-Law God makes me a better son-in-law.

Favor

I want to close this chapter on the Father-in-Law God with a discussion of favor. I am talking about the favor of God. As Christians, most of us would love for God to like us, not just love us. I am writing this chapter during the holiday season. Many of us have visited or been visited by family members. There are some family members you might like more than others due to their personality, choices, or their history with you or other family members. The ones you like have favor with you, while the ones you like less—though you may love them deeply as well—you can say have less favor with you.

I will use an analogy that can develop your understanding of the favor of God. Many of us who marry and become parents along the way will understand this analogy. However, even if you are not a parent, I think this analogy will still work to help you understand this.

Suppose one of your children has a unique talent in sports, music, engineering—any unique talent. You take your child to a coach or leader in their area of talent. This person agrees your child is gifted or talented and sacrificially supports your child. Regardless of this person's personality, characteristics, or qualities, you are going to like or favor this person. This is really simple: When someone loves who you love, you will favor them.

Look at this from another direction. Say it is the same child and you take him or her to a coach or leader who excels in coaching or leading others in the area of your child's talent or giftedness. But then the person chooses to put your child down and discourages them, even shames them. Now, how do you feel toward this person? To say the least, you would not like (favor) them very much, would you?

Notice that the second person did not love who you loved, so you did not have favor for them. The first person loved who you loved (your child), and they found favor with you.

Now, go back to you and your marriage. Suppose for a moment that God really likes/loves His child (your spouse). If you treat your spouse well by loving, serving and encouraging him or her it is quite possible God could like you because of the way you serve your spouse. Conversely, if you treat your spouse (His child He deeply loves) poorly, discourage him or her, or are consistently unkind to him or her, you might find yourself lacking in the favor of God in your life. I know God loves when I do laundry, dishes, or otherwise help my wife, and when I encourage and praise her. I honestly believe I have many blessings in my life because of God's favor on me because of how I love to bless His daughter, Lisa.

Having a Father-in-Law God is not a bad thing: It is actually a wonderful thing. He is omnipresent, so it does not matter what country or city I am in, He is with me. He is all-knowing, so He can constantly give me revelation and wisdom in how to better love and serve my wife. He is also amazingly gracious when I make mistakes with His daughter, my wife.

I hope you are encouraged by having God as your father-in-law. Having His expectations, His empowerment to be a servant to my spouse, and knowing one day I will face Him for my actions and behaviors is comforting and motivates me to love and serve Lisa all the days I am privileged to have her as my wife.

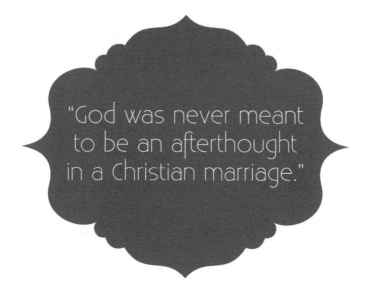

"God was never meant to be an afterthought in a Christian marriage."

Jesus as Servant

As Christians, the ultimate goal of our entire lives is to be like Jesus. To walk, talk, believe, feel, and be like Jesus in our daily life—this is our inner ambition. This ambition is also shared with the Holy Spirit. As God, He comes into us for the sole purpose of creating the nature of Christ in us.

Decade after decade, marriage provides ample opportunities to be Christlike. After all, ultimately, that is the Father's primary objective for marriage—to make us Christlike. Have you ever wondered why you are married to someone quite different from you? This is not meant to irritate us, but rather to kill our flesh and help us become Christlike as we die in the process of loving this amazing being; our spouse.

Now, if we are going to be like Jesus, especially in our marriage (the true testing ground for our faith, beliefs, and what truly lurks in our hearts), we need to really understand the servant nature and calling of Jesus.

Jesus, just like Adam and Jeremiah (and probably you and I), had a calling and purpose created before we were created. You and I were created and given life to solve a problem here on earth. We have a destiny to touch lives in our time zone in world history. Some of us find our purpose from the Father, some fight it, some never seek it, and sadly, some die without achieving their purpose.

In Genesis, God said there was no man to work the Garden (problem) before he created man (solution). He said it was not good for Adam to be alone (problem), so He created the solution (woman). Jeremiah said God knew him before He created him to be a proclaimer of God's message (Isaiah 49:5):

"And now the Lord says—
 he who formed me in the womb to be his servant
to bring Jacob back to him
 and gather Israel to himself,
for I am honored in the eyes of the Lord
 and my God has been my strength—"

There is an echo of this being a solution for all of us in our heart of hearts. We are not the problem; we are to be the solutions on planet Earth as well as in our marriage. When I am a servant husband, I am a solution to my wife and family.

Look back at Jesus as it pertains to this issue of being a servant. We get glimpses of this idea of Jesus in the Old Testament many years before Mary carried Jesus in the womb.

In Isaiah 52:13 and 53:11, Jesus is called a "servant" or "righteous servant" before He came as a man. Also, in Zechariah, Jesus is called, "my servant, the branch (Zechariah 3:8). Isaiah 53 talks about Jesus serving even through the disfigurement of His body. He was disfigured through the crucifixion for our sin, not His.

You will not necessarily be disfigured through marriage, but you will experience dying to yourself and being transformed more into the image of Christ as you and I serve our spouse. This is why I love the message of Isaiah 53, that after Jesus suffered, there would be many blessings.

After he has suffered,
    he will see the light of life and be satisfied;
by his knowledge my righteous servant will justify many,
    and he will bear their iniquities. (Isaiah 53:11, NIV)

Again, you will be crucified in marriage, not literally, but your flesh will die. As you die, you are blessed; and not only you, but your spouse, children, fellow church members, friends, and your community. All can be touched by you becoming more Christlike through the process called marriage. Just remember, God created this process and He is glorified through your life of service.

Just as a sidenote, it is interesting to see the heart of the woman God chose to bear Jesus. As God looked throughout the tribe of Judah for a woman, He found Mary. Look at Mary's response to the angels' proclamation to her that she would have a son: "'I am the Lord's servant,'" Mary answered. "'May your word to me be fulfilled'" (Luke 1:38, NIV).

This servant DNA was so powerful in Mary that when she was confronted by an angel in a dramatic supernatural encounter, she defined herself as a servant, "I am the Lord's servant" (Luke 1:38, NIV). Jesus not only had a day in and day out heavenly servant model in the Father, He also had a ready earthly servant model in his mother in both her heart and behavior. She was a servant giving birth to *the* Servant. Mary also described herself as a servant in Luke 1:48 (NIV): "He has been mindful of the humble state of his servant. From now on all generations will call me blessed." She really did see herself as a servant.

We will explore Jesus' teachings on being a servant more deeply in the pages ahead, but it is important to first look at how the rest of the New Testament describes Jesus as a servant.

In Acts we read: "The God of Abraham, Isaac and Jacob, the God of our fathers, has glorified his servant Jesus" (Acts 3:13, NIV). Acts 3:26 (NIV) continues: "When God raised up his servant, he sent him first to you to bless you by turning each of you from your wicked ways." Acts 4:27 (NIV) calls Jesus "holy servant Jesus."

Paul also writes about Jesus being a servant on several occasions. In Romans 15:8 (NIV), Paul says: "For I tell you that Christ has become a servant of the Jews on behalf of Gods truth, so that the promises made to the patriarchs might be confirmed." In Philippians Paul says, "He made himself nothing by taking the very nature of a servant, being made in human likeness" (Philippians 2:7, NIV).

Jesus also said of Himself in Matthew 20:28 (NIV): "The Son of Man did not come to be served, but to serve, and to give his life as a ransom for many."

Jesus was not only described as a servant in both the Old and New Testaments; He Himself lived a life of a servant.

During His earthly ministry, Jesus taught about serving on a number of occasions. So often we find ourselves living in a secular world. Even at church, some of our pastors have bought into the secular notion of leadership and its spirit, expecting to be served rather than be a servant of the body of Christ. I find that going back to exactly what Jesus Himself said best clarifies the true heart of being a servant. A few of His teachings on serving remind us of Jesus's thoughts on this subject, so are particularly valuable to explore. As we walk through these passages, remind yourself that we are applying these principles to marriage and how we can think and feel about our service toward our spouses.

One of the most famous teachings of Jesus about serving is taught in several scriptures: Matthew 20:26, 23:11-12, and; Mark 9:35, 10:43-44. In Matthew 20 (which we will explore more deeply in the pages ahead) we find a story of a mother of two disciples making a request of Jesus that he put her sons in a place of honor and esteem above the other disciples, specifically at His right and left in His kingdom. As the story proceeds, Jesus makes this famous statement in verses 26 and 27 (NIV): "Whoever wants to become great among you must be your servant, and whoever wants to be first must be your slave." It is interesting that He did not rebuke the idea of someone wanting to be great. He just shifted the idea of the process.

You come to marriage from a vastly different place when you accept the calling to serve your spouse rather than to rule them. You also experience two very different outcomes. A servant will become great in the eyes of those he or she serves. A less than positive-hearted person will desire to be seen as great without the service record required to actually be seen that way.

An example of this difference is a father who demands respect because of position— "I'm your father"—as opposed to another who serves and can with a clear conscience inspire others to "follow my service and serve well." This difference is also about servant marriage versus secular marriage, even if both spouses are Christians.

In another setting in Matthew 13, Jesus reiterates this idea of serving. It comes during a teaching He gives about the Pharisees. After warning his listeners not to be like those who seek positions and titles from men, He says in verses 11-12 (NIV): "The greatest among you will be your servant. For those who exalt themselves will be humbled, and those who humble themselves will be exalted."

In Mark 10, Jesus retells the story of James and John's mother's request with a slightly different emphasis. In verses 43 to 44 (NIV) He says: "Not so with you. Instead, whoever wants to become great among you must be your servant, and whoever wants to be first must be *slave of all*" (NIV, italics added). The slight variation in the story is the word "all." These ideas of being called and willing to actually be a servant of everyone strike deep in the heart, and are at the foundation of servant marriage. Jesus actually talked to the disciples about the exact point of being a servant just a chapter earlier, in Mark 9:33-35. This time the disciples were talking among themselves about who would be the greatest: "They came to Capernaum. When he was in the house, he asked them, 'What were you arguing about on the road?' But they kept quiet because on the way they had argued about who was the greatest. Sitting down, Jesus called the Twelve and said, 'Anyone who wants to be first must be the very last, and the servant of *all*'" (NIV, italics added).

Again, He uses the word "*all*." Whether "all" means everyone all the time or all of those present, I am not sure, however, in application it does not make much difference. Jesus is clearly saying greatness is in service to one another. I cannot think of a better place to purely desire to be great than in your marriage. If you are great in your marriage by serving, you have created an environment by example (like my wife has) that your spouse will honor over time and hopefully duplicate. By so doing, our God will gain a whole bloodline of servant-hearted spouses demonstrating His kingdom-heartedness to each generation.

I guess this could be equally true if you are Christians, but secular in your marriage concept. You could believe that greatness is determined by position and this position is of one to be served. You can create a secular marriage mindset in a Christian context. You can be a Christian spouse who wants to be served and dominate from that position and establish that bloodline. In such cases, their lineage will only be freed when at least one spouse receives a revelation of servant-minded marriage and acts on it to demolish the secular mindset curse.

Being a servant in a marriage is the only way to be great in a marriage. Serving one's spouse kills selfishness and self-centeredness—what we call our "flesh." By dying to ourselves in marriage, we prepare ourselves for the selfless task of parenting. In conferences I kiddingly say, "What God cannot kill in you in your marriage, He'll allow your children to finish off." You get the point. I think marriage is an awesome opportunity to die. Serving is all about voluntarily dying to our preferences and growing in honor and appreciation of our spouses.

Optimally, it is best when both spouses in a marriage understand their calling to serve. When this happens, the children get to see two different personalities serving each other. This is the most beautiful and healthy way to grow up, for sure.

As we go through the next few examples, I want you to see who was tempting Jesus to bite the apple of superiority and monarchial ideas, and His consistent reaction to these ideas.

The very first temptation aimed toward Jesus to be a secular king and ruler came immediately after His baptism by John. You may well be familiar with the scene in Matthew 3:13-17 (NIV):

¹³Then Jesus came from Galilee to the Jordan to be baptized by John. ¹⁴ But John tried to deter him, saying, "I need to be baptized by you, and do you come to me?" ¹⁵ Jesus replied, "Let it be so now; it is proper for us to do this to fulfill all righteousness." Then John consented. ¹⁶ As soon as Jesus was baptized, he went up out of the water. At that moment heaven was opened, and he saw the Spirit of God descending like a dove and alighting on him.¹⁷ And a voice from heaven said, "This is my Son, whom I love; with him I am well pleased."

The Spirit descends and the Father speaks the famous words of encouragement to the Son: "This is my Son, whom I love; with him I am well pleased" (Matthew 3:17, NIV).

Now remember, Satan knows God's voice and knows the presence of the Spirit. Perhaps above all others, he knew this was really happening and that Jesus was the chosen one of God—God's Son. In chapter 4, Jesus is led by the Spirit to fast for forty days and nights.

On this part, the Devil, after attempting to tempt Jesus twice already, tries a third time. He offers to make Jesus a secular monarch. Here is that account:

⁸ Again, the devil took him to a very high mountain and showed him all the kingdoms of the world and their splendor. ⁹ "All this I will give you," he said, "if you will bow down and worship me."

¹⁰ Jesus said to him, "Away from me, Satan! For it is written: 'Worship the Lord your God, and serve him only.'"

¹¹ Then the devil left him, and angels came and attended him.   Matthew 4:8-11 (NIV)

By rejecting this request, Jesus was also rejecting the temptation to be a secular ruler. Truth be known, this same idea is what caused Satan to be cast out of heaven and placed on planet Earth. The second temptation for Jesus to act as a secular king came through a mother of two disciples. Now, I do not think this mother in Matthew 20 had an unclean or ill motive. Like any mother, I am sure she just wanted the best for her sons. She heard the message of the kingdom, but only had only one experiential reference point for kingdom, which was Roman domination. She asked Jesus to act like a monarch, at least to a point, or to establish a secular order in which her sons would be preeminent over the other disciples.

Jesus is consistent in His character, even to this well-meaning mother, and He rejected playing the role of a monarch, deflecting this to the Father. Jesus rejected monarchial rule with His disciples.

The king idea was pushed on Jesus a third time by a crowd of people upon His triumphal entry into Jerusalem. Here is the account of this episode:

³⁷ When he came near the place where the road goes down the Mount of Olives, the whole crowd of disciples began joyfully to praise God in loud voices for all the miracles they had seen:
> **³⁸** "Blessed is the king who comes in the name of the Lord!"
> "Peace in heaven and glory in the highest!"

³⁹ Some of the Pharisees in the crowd said to Jesus, "Teacher, rebuke your disciples!"

⁴⁰ "I tell you," he replied, "if they keep quiet, the stones will cry out."

⁴¹ As he approached Jerusalem and saw the city, he wept over it **⁴²** and said, "If you, even you, had only known on this day what would bring you peace—but now it is hidden from your eyes. **⁴³** The days will come upon you when your enemies will build an embankment against you and encircle you and hem you in on every side. **⁴⁴** They will dash you to the ground, you and the children within your walls. They will not leave one stone on another, because you did not recognize the time of God's coming to you." (Luke 19:37-44, NIV)

I am sure that if a crowd of people were calling many of us to be king, we might well be tempted to think about the idea. However, happy to be a servant, Jesus did not appear to struggle here with the crowd. Jesus's character and reaction to ideas of monarchy are consistent; He rejects them and reiterates that He is a servant.

In your marriage, you too will be tempted to grab hold of the notion that you are to be served, especially if you are a man. The devil will tempt you to rule over your spouse. At some level, of course, you have to believe you are innately worthy of such a position to bite that apple. Your religious group may also subscribe to a religious version of this by posing to you the Bible verse that says a man is to be the head of his wife, like Christ is head of the church. The secular interpretation of this suggests that as a man, you are to rule over or dominate your wife. The scripture they are referencing actually says that

Jesus is a servant head of the church, and He laid down His life for her. So, if your religious group tempts you to dominate or rule over your spouse, be careful. Doing so will rob you of spiritual growth and the blessings of being a servant to your spouse, regardless of whether you are a man or a woman.

The crowd or culture will also scream out to you to not let anyone walk all over you; to demand respect. Some cultures will even promote hitting one's spouse. The culture has always aligned itself with monarchy thinking, but that is not the culture of the kingdom. We are servants of the Most High God. Being a servant of God and of our spouse is not such a bad thing. Look at a few people below who God called His servants.

Throughout Genesis, Abraham calls Himself a servant, but in Genesis 26:24, God calls Abraham His servant. Moses similarly calls Himself a servant throughout Exodus. However, in Numbers and throughout Scripture, God calls Moses a servant—and a faithful servant at that. Caleb was also called a servant by God. David called himself a servant and God Himself agreed, calling David His servant (1 Chronicles 17:4-7). So, "servant" does not seem to be too bad of a title, and is shared with Jesus, Abraham, Moses, Caleb, David, and many more. Actually, I would rather be called a servant by God than be given any other title by anyone else. God seems to honor those He calls a servant.

Remember that Jesus was called a servant before He was even born. He lived a life of a servant while on earth. He taught about being a servant and resisted monarchial thinking. We can also see some of God's favorite people were called servants as well.

So, what will be written about you and I? Paul says each of us is a written epistle. So, what would be written about you and I in our marriage? What would our children "read" as they watched our marriage? Would they have seen (or are they seeing) two people duking it out to see who will rule the family, or two servants living with the Father as king of their marriage? Being a servant might not be any more popular today than it was in Jesus's day.

The devil is still the devil, so we know he still wants to pull us into monarchial thinking. He does not do this because he thinks it is right or best. He knows it is not the way the kingdom of heaven works. (After all, he was punished for believing such an idea.) He does this because he hates us and wants what is worst for ourselves and our marriage.

The world will never change. Even the last book of the Bible talks about kings and world "leaders," not servants. So, the world will call to you to lead in your marriage and be served—not to serve. These two contrasting ideas will battle throughout time.

Only God's voice calls to each one of us, as believers in Christ Jesus, to die to ourselves—regardless of gender, wealth, academic or other accomplishments—and serve Him and our spouse.

I love serving my spouse, Lisa. Admittedly, it took some revelation and obedience to get me to where I began enjoying my role and calling to serve Lisa, but the blessings of doing so have made this more than worth it. As you and your spouse walk through your journey with the Lord in servant marriage, you will have many chapters to write of dying to selfishness, being right, being most important, and a whole host of other really bad ideas. You will have many more chapters about the blessings of servant marriage not only for you and your spouse, but also for your children, grandchildren, and others who had a front row seat to see your servant marriage.

"You come to marriage from a vastly different place when you accept the calling to serve your spouse rather than to rule them."

Attitude

As I think back to my New Year's Eve date with my wife (I will describe later in the book), I talk about the food at the restaurant, and then segued into the food we serve our spouse. The aspect of that evening I did not talk about was the service. I do not know about you, but occasionally I have been to restaurants, even nice restaurants, and the service was substandard, to say the least. (Admittedly, I may be even more sensitive than most, because when I was in Bible college, I was a waiter in a nice restaurant that prided itself on service.) Sometimes it has even seemed as if the mere act of me asking for something bothered the waiter or waitress. On the flip side of this, you can also be in an average restaurant with average food and have great service and the service makes the overall experience very positive. Even in a decent restaurant with good food, the service can greatly diminish or enhance the overall experience.

Recently, we went out to a restaurant with our children and a couple of their college friends. The waitress was great. She stayed on top of refilling drinks and she got the order right for all six of us—exactly as we asked—without having written it down. We all talked about how good the service was as we left. In another example, Lisa and I went out to a local restaurant after work one night. The waiter was so friendly to both of us and so competent, we went back again just because of the service we received. The attitude in which service is given has a significant impact on those being served.

When Jesus washed His disciples' feet, could you imagine Him saying: "Boys, line up! I have to splash water on your disgusting feet to make a point. I am doing this only because my Father wants me to do it. Hurry! Let's get this done." In the Bible, not once do you see Jesus serving with a *bad* attitude. I think this is because He embraced His calling to serve humanity (as we explored earlier). Out of His acceptance, He had a good attitude in serving us humans.

In this chapter, I want to highlight some key characteristics you will see in yourself as you embrace servant marriage. I am going to touch upon common attitudes of someone who moves through being served to the one who is serving. As you read, keep in mind the stages of grief (we will cover in Chapter 8): shock, demand, anger, bargaining, sadness, and acceptance. As we move toward fully embracing our calling to serve our spouse, we can have different attitudes. You can see the attitudes you have had in the past—even the attitudes you have now—when you say out loud, "I am a servant to my spouse." The emotions you experience when you make this confession will tell you where you are. If you still have strong emotions resistant to your confession of being a servant, the attitude we first discussed may show up. However, if you are really good with being your spouse's servant "til death do you part," then the second part of the chapter will feel familiar to you.

As you go through these various attitudes, I want you to know each is normal, and any attitude can change as the heart embraces its calling from God to serve your spouse. So do not feel bad if you identify an attitude you do not like about yourself; it can change into a wonderful attitude over time.

Also, as we have discussed throughout this book, stay focused on you. You will be really tempted to see the less-than-wonderful attitudes of your spouse. My experience is, I can only grow as a servant as I focus on my own quality and attitude of service, not my spouse's.

Also note that as believers in Christ Jesus, we are 100 percent responsible for our own attitudes. We definitely do not want to blame anyone, including our spouses, for the current attitude we have or past attitude we had about being a servant.

We also have the Holy Spirit to help us see our attitudes and give us the power to transform any of our less-than-wonderful attitudes toward our calling to serve to more pleasing ones. The journey of transformation does not have to move from point to point as we embrace our high calling to serve.

Resistant

This is the attitude I see a lot from both men and women, but more men than women. Often they go to churches where the men are told it is biblical to dominate and bully their wives into "submission." (Interestingly enough, I have never spoken to men or women who teach this who are actually submitted to real spiritual authority themselves.)

The resistant attitude is often held by those who, deep in their heart, still long to be served. Such people want excellent service from their spouse, but are internally resistant to serve their spouse. They will do what they feel comfortable doing or what gives them a gold star publicly, but express an attitude of resistance when the spouse asks for something outside their pre-determined mindset—say of how they might contribute to the household or their spouse as a person.

Those with a resistant attitude are still honestly struggling with embracing the death part of marriage. They really do not get that if two are to become one, the two have to die in many ways to make this new creature (a triune marriage). Their understanding of the two shall become one flesh idea is that the other person will become like them and then they will both be wonderful. This pride can be toxic for a marriage for sure.

Resistance is normal when you are walking into a knife. Your rights are being cut. Your entitlement, your role as a secular leader, and in some cases even wrong theology, must be sacrificed for you to become a servant husband or wife.

This resistance is not gender specific. I have seen women express their hate for their calling to serve their husband through anger, silence, physical issues, withholding sex, withholding praise. They have to die in many ways to serve the husband they have not served in decades. When our flesh is in a place of dying, it is not always quiet, nor is it without some stench.

Resistance lets us know—at least—that hopefully we are moving toward becoming a servant to our spouse. We might not internally like this idea, but deep down inside us, we know it is God's will and desire for us to not only be servants to our spouses, but to be excellent servants to our spouses.

Resentful

"Why do I have to?" "Why me?" "Why can't they?" "I have needs, too!" "I deserve to be able to do . . . have . . . be . . . " When you start feeling or expressing some of these attitudes, you might be expressing resentment over the fact that you are a servant to your spouse. When you took that ring and said, "I do," you made a covenant to be a servant to your spouse.

Sometimes (or should I say usually?) service is extremely inconvenient; whether due to bad timing or conflict with our own agenda. Being a servant is inconvenient, so resentment can build up while you serve if you are not careful.

Every Saturday, I wake up before my wife just because I require less sleep to function. There is usually laundry to do, dishes to wash, garbage to be taken out, or any number of other things to do, even if only just feeding the dog. I like Saturdays as well, especially if I am writing a book. Usually, I can get a chapter or two knocked out before we need to go anywhere.

Every Saturday I have a choice. I could do all the tasks I listed above on my own, or choose to resent that they were not already done by Lisa or someone else. I can project things that would not be true of my wife or her intentions. I can resent that "I have to" instead of "I get to" serve in that manner, at that time, or I can just have a good attitude. Usually, my attitude is: It is my house. I am just going to get it done so I can move on with things I would like to get done today. Usually.

You see, my wife works alongside me every day. Lisa runs all aspects: conferences, publishing, counseling center, and more. She puts in as many hours as I do at Heart to Heart Counseling Center. If I were tempted toward resentment, I would look for something (typically small) that was not done. This would be silly of me. Lisa is an extremely hard worker at the office, at home, and at the office. I would rather look at all she does and just celebrate how blessed I am. Then I have no problem with whatever is left to do.

I received a revelation that really helped me along the road of marriage, and it destroys any possible resentment. The revelation was simple: God gave Adam the

Garden to work. Eve was only supposed to be a helper. The way I look at it is this: I was created stronger, bigger, and to need less sleep (but more food); so I can do more around the house. It is my job. If she helps, she is doing her part. This insight makes me very grateful for every dish washed or put away, clothes done, garbage taken out, and more, because without her help, I would have had to do it. This attitude killed any resentment and made me grateful for what Lisa does.

Resentment often arises due to some sense of entitlement or thinking, *this is beneath me, I am more important than this*, or *this isn't my job*. It creeps in over time. Sometimes we do not even know it is there until we are asked to go above and beyond what we thought it meant to be a good spouse.

I know some guys who, when their serving cuts into their time for watching sports, running, or their golf game, respond by acting like children and showing resentment to their spouse for days. Conversely, a woman might feel put out by her spouse's desire to have sex in the middle of the day, or to have her pick up something he needs that he forgot (again), and harbor resentment toward him for days.

All of us get that twinge or feeling of "this isn't what I planned for the day" at times. How we respond to it makes all the difference. I am a servant of the Most High God. I do not get to decide my day. When I remind myself of this, I can usually perk up and maintain a good attitude.

Watch resentment carefully because it grows slowly from resentment of the call to be a servant to resentment of the task of serving to resentment of one's spouse. Once you move into resentment of your spouse and the work it takes to maintain and serve a spouse, you are getting your heart into a place that can be problematic.

This process is similar to that of owning a puppy. Puppies are incredibly cute and cuddly, and their messes are small at the beginning (the honeymoon stage). Then the dog's messes start getting bigger, more expensive, or personal (on favorite shoes and so on). Then the dog requires baths, grooming, medical appointments, vaccines, and needs to be watched for vacation (increasing maintenance). You can accept that having a dog requires a lot of work, or you can resent the work the dog requires. If you choose to resent the work, you can begin to resent the dog.

Once you start resenting the dog, the dog becomes a symbol of work to you. When you see the dog, you no longer see the cute puppy, you see work. When the dog equals work, you resent the dog.

The same is true of our spouses. At first, they are cute, but then they are a little work, and then they are more work and more personally expensive. You can accept the work and love the person of your spouse. However, you can also resent the work and then resent your spouse because when you see him or her, all you see is the work they are for you (resentment) rather than the glorious creature God made them to be that you have the privilege to know and serve. The choice is ours, of course.

Our attitude is 100 percent our responsibility. I can never blame or scapegoat Lisa for my attitude. If I see her as a gift and maintain her and the household as a "get to" rather than a "have to," I can daily escape the trap of the enemy to behold my wife in some unkind manner.

This is a very important heart check for all of us who are married. If our hearts move to a place where our spouse is now a symbol of work, we have moved into a dangerous position. Once a person becomes a symbol of work, you will respond, react, and behave totally differently toward them. Your spouse in a servant marriage needs to stay a person.

Yes, marriage is work. Yes, having children and raising a family is work. As a Western Christian, this is the glorious work for which I volunteered. I was not forced by anyone to marry Lisa. I choose this work.

Just like those who choose the military or some other vocation, we choose the opportunity, and all opportunities are work. I need to keep the person of Lisa and her value at the forefront of my mind. Focusing on the facts that she was "died for" and is the royal daughter of God inoculates me from the enemy's plan to sow seeds of resentment into the sands of our marriage.

Fair

Most of us like to have things fair. You know, if the pizza or cake has six slices, we both get three. However, absolute fairness is impossible in life with humans. If life were truly fair, we would all spend eternity in a very hot place.

Christ did a very unfair thing by taking on humanity, serving while alive, and in His death, giving us eternal life to be as much of a blessing as we can in our time on this planet, due to His Spirit inside us.

There is nothing so innately good or wonderful about me that would demand my wife's service toward me these almost thirty years of marriage. I am not innately worthy of that—not one of us is. Marriage is not fair in any way, shape, or form.

Marriage is intentionally designed to cause you pain and inconvenience in order to teach you to love your spouse unselfishly. And by so loving them, you become Christlike. This process is not fair, but it is necessary to become Christlike in many ways—to lay down our lives for our spouses. Remember; this is love.

When this attitude of wanting fairness comes knocking at your door, be careful. The desire for fairness will cause you to create a very destructive habit that will sabotage you and keep you from being an awesome servant in your marriage. The habit fairness wants to create in you is that of keeping score. (As if any human can really, in any way, weigh the complexities of the wide variety of actions in any relationship and somehow tabulate fairness.)

Keeping score is a cancer to your success as a servant. Like all the other attitudes, it starts off a little slow, with: *It's not fair that* _____, or *It's not fair that you get to* _____. Then you get into a task that you are not equipped by God to do: You assess and measure what each of you do and keep score as to who is doing more. The problem is, you can only use a subjective scale, so whatever you are doing for the marriage or family, it has at least equal or more important value than what your husband or wife is doing that day, week, month, or year.

Once you start keeping score, you will be tempted to look at your spouse through a false set of lenses that keep him or her constantly in a position one down from you. Over time, this attitude will lead you to a potentially fatal stage of the cancer of fairness: disrespect.

Once you conclude that your spouse is not carrying his or her weight (which is where a false sense of fairness will inevitably lead), you will move toward disrespecting them as a person. It starts with you thinking your spouse does not respect that you do not do this or that, or that your spouse does not appreciate this or that which you do. Inevitably, you begin to move toward wholehearted disrespect of them. Your judgments become personal: *My spouse is lazy, incompetent, disorganized, ungrateful, insensitive, and so on.*

The attitude of fairness is so seductive at the beginning. I want you to know fairness is a cancer. If you start this, it can ultimately culminate in the destruction of your marriage, or at least make your marriage significantly less happy than if you were both servants who understood life and marriage were not fair (not even supposed to be fair). You must both sacrifice your lives for the marriage to be awesome.

To kill fairness you have to tear out some roots of ideas that can lead you down this awful path.

1. Fairness does not exist.

I do not know who the author of the book *Life Should Be Fair* is, but he or she is responsible for global deception, for sure. This world will never be fair. I am not even sure fair exists in heaven. (We know there are elders in heaven. Why is it fair that they be elders?)

As an idea, fair cannot and will not ever exist in the world. Fair cannot be achieved—ever. Fairness is a total illusion of the soul. Fairness does not exist in God's heart, like mercy and grace through Christ Jesus. He is a just God, but fair is a human contract we are in no way capable of measuring in relationship to each other.

You want to banish the very idea of fair to a place outside your marriage and family. The children in our family have occasionally spouted out, "That's not fair" (as all children do at some point). We typically responded with something like this: "Who lied to you that life was fair? If it ever did get fair, your lifestyle would decrease significantly."

So if you were ever lied to about Santa Claus or the Easter Bunny, or told that life is fair, I am sad for you. However, fairness has never and will never exist. (If this hurts you or angers you, read the chapter on grief.)

If you still believe in fair you will be playing all kinds of childish games to make your life and marriage happier.

Accepting that fair does not exist and that you do not even want fair can liberate you quite a bit in your life and marriage.

2. I cannot measure fairness.

The hardest part of accepting that fairness does not, cannot, and will never exist is accepting that you do not even have any capability to measure fairness. I have four degrees on my wall. I have written just over fifty books or workbooks. I have several other accolades. Still, I am in no way capable of measuring fairness.

I cannot quantify Lisa's insights, contributions, and effort in our home, family, or business. I cannot calculate or measure these things in any way. I would have to be totally delusional to think I could ever compare her emotional support for a child to anything I do.

We are deceived at our core if we think we can ever create a measure of fairness in a marriage. There is no way to measure something that does not and will never exist. When we believe in fairness we want to measure fairness. When we do not believe in fairness, we are not even tempted to measure it or get trapped into a conversation about fairness (or the Easter Bunny).

However, trying to measure fairness is an indication you might well believe in the non-existent idea of fairness. You know yourself that just being honest with your struggle can help you walk free in your servant marriage.

3. My life is not about fairness, but service.

The struggle with those who believe in fairness is its demand on you to give it your allegiance. Fairness or faith in fairness is almost like pledging allegiance to a flag with no country.

Fairness demands a portion of your mind, will, and emotions (especially emotions) . . . and your life. Your life becomes about counting what you are doing in the marriage, or worse yet, what your spouse is or is not doing.

Fairness can call you to a cause outside or inside of your marriage. Inside your marriage you campaign for fairness as if it exists. If you give your heart to things being fair in life or in marriage, you might sentence yourself to discontentment for as long as your faith is being used in that false manner.

4. My Savior shows me that service is more valued than any false sense of fairness.

Jesus is our example. He never taught us that life was fair. He left glory (not fair) to become a man (not fair). He served endlessly while walking on earth (not fair). He was falsely accused (not fair), crucified (not fair). He continues to serve in intercession for us (not fair).

When you look at Christ, I think it is radically clear He placed a very high value on service. He lived life as a servant to others. He served His bride—the church—in death and resurrection. Jesus placed no value on fairness.

Jesus knew the ailments of humanity better than anyone. He paid for them in full. He knew the future of the world would hold wars and famines. He told us as much. He did not come to make our lives fair by any standard. He came to seek the lost and gave us eternal life and a mission: Disciple believers and bring non-believers into the household of our Father.

Truly, if Jesus was not about fairness but about abundant service, both in word and deed, this should give us a clue to what He values most.

When you misbelieve in fairness you give fairness a value in your heart. This value of fairness can grow over the years and even surpass the value of service or even the value of your spouse.

When fairness (which again, does not exist) becomes a value in your heart, the consequences are real. When we believe a lie, we behave a lie, and that lie has consequences for us and those we love.

When we value fairness over service (which does exist) we can consternate ourselves. We can also put undo strain on our marriage because our spouse will rarely measure up to our concept of fair when we hold to the false notion of fairness.

5. The service my spouse will need of me will never be fair nor measurable, but it is guaranteed to kill me to be like Christ.

As I see it, service has several objectives. Service gives us a spiritual workout. When we serve we get spiritually stronger. Serving is like lifting spiritual weights or going for a spiritual jog.

Service also kills our flesh (as we have emphasized). Pride, self-will, and a number of other fleshly characteristics have to take a back seat when we serve. So service ultimately makes us like Jesus, the ultimate servant.

As we embrace service we are actively embracing a Christlike lifestyle; a lifestyle that leads us directly into His nature of a servant. Actually, the sooner we embrace the reality of this calling to our spouse the easier marriage becomes.

6. Christlikeness is God's goal for me in marriage.

Now that we know the goal of God is to make us in the image of His Son, we know that the power of the Holy Spirit is being actualized to highlight that we must die and give us the power to kill our flesh to walk in the Spirit toward our spouse. I say, "Let's get it on!"

We must not hesitate, procrastinate, or do any other "ate." We must agree with the goal. We must be able to say to God: "I agree with your agenda to change me into Christ's likeness on earth so that during the little amount of time I have here, people will experience you."

You see, when we agree with the goal of Christlikeness, we are in agreement with God's plan for our lives. Then

He can use everything, but especially our marriage, to bring us to maturity as His servants—not just churchgoers—but servants who go to church. A servant is the goal of my God for me. I absolutely know this to be true, and embrace the death of me so more of Him can be seen.

If you can plant these truths into your being you will forever be free from the tormenting cancer of fairness. If, however, you maintain any of the opposite ideas (listed below), you and fairness will have a long, hard journey together.

1. Fairness does exist.
2. I alone can measure fairness.
3. My life is about fairness.
4. False fairness has more value than His death for me.
5. My service should be fair and equal toward my spouse.
6. My marriage should make me happy and be fair.

When we believe lies, the fruits of that lie will be in our lives. When we believe the truth this also bears fruit in our lives. If you have the cancer of fairness growing in you, this attitude can be challenging to remove. But in Christ, you can and will be free to be a servant who does not even want to keep score, with no fantasies about fairness.

Acceptance

Acceptance is a great attitude to have as a servant in a marriage. Acceptance is, "I am here to serve you," "I was created to serve you," "serving you honors God, myself, you, and our future generations," and, "I am a servant."

Wow, when you get this level of acceptance you are going to really enjoy your servant marriage. You see, I am a servant before any other title I have earned or been given. "This is your servant, how can I help you?" This is what I want my children to learn from me in marriage. This is the DNA I want in my family tree for generations.

It is the heart of God to have servant children serving one another. When we accept this, the fight is over with man's fleshly issues that arise in and harm marriages.

Acceptance of being a servant is a freeing attitude. This attitude takes you into a lifestyle of humility and gratefulness in the process. For me, it was a process to be a servant rather than just being helpful here and there. I am a servant. It is not what I do, it is who I am as I have embraced and accepted that I am a servant. It has led me to the final attitude I want to share with you.

Learner

When I am given a task or challenge, I want to do a great job with it. To do a great job—even if it is only a hobby—I have to learn and stay a learner. If we want to become awesome servants, we have to remain in a position of heart as a learner of our spouses. When I remain a learner I can be a servant to Lisa throughout our marriage.

Marriage brings changes over the years. You move from apartment to house to having children, to having children in school, to having kids in college, the children's weddings, grandchildren, aging, and more. Each stage reassures us that, as servants we will grow, learn, and adapt. Also, the person we serve changes. What they enjoyed as a young person (ice cream or vigorous exercise) might change as they age (salads and rest).

As a learner, you ask questions both about serving on the perimeter as well as serving the person. As I ask Lisa about her, I learn her. I ask her for her perceptions about the perimeter because she sees things I do not see, and vice versa. I keep learning. If you have an attitude of a learner and maintain it, you are guaranteed to grow in your calling and ability to fulfill the calling to service.

As a Christian you have an endless supply of patience, kindness, goodness, and self-control flowing through your heart. God has not called you to serve your spouse for decades without fully giving you what you need to fulfill your unique and glorious mission.

Remember the mission you have already chosen is long, challenging, and full of joy, peace, ups and downs, and unpredictable events unique to your marriage and family.

You are not alone on your magnificent quest. You have God, the Word of God, an amazing spouse, your spiritual leaders and community, family, friendships, and unlimited tools to read online and in books over the decades.

You can do this. You are a servant of the Most High God. As you travel faithfully decade after decade, hear the echoes of your Father and Father-in-Law God desiring to say words your heart longs to hear.

"Well done my good and faithful servant."

"Marriage is intentionally designed to cause you pain and inconvenience in order to teach you to love your spouse unselfishly."

What Food Are You Serving?

Eating is a wonderful part of our lives. I love going to restaurants that serve meals created with excellence. It does not matter if it is a burger, filet mignon, french fries, or lobster, if it is done with excellence, I really enjoy the effort, sacrifice, wisdom, and creativity it takes to serve such an item.

I am getting hungry even thinking about how awesome food is. Last night was New Years, and I went to one of my favorite local restaurants here in Colorado Springs. We were impressed as always with the welcome, the service, the presentation, and the taste of the food. This was an overall fantastic night with my wife Lisa.

Why am I talking so much about food in a marriage book? Good question! In a marriage of several decades, you "eat" (so to speak) so much of what your spouse is serving during the marriage.

Your spouse's service toward you is impactful on your life but the food itself can be anywhere on the spectrum, from awful—even toxic—to amazing and fortifying. The fruit from your spouse's attitudes, beliefs, behaviors, and motivations are all foods you get served every day.

Figuratively, we eat from and are greatly impacted by the lives of our spouse. Who they are, what they bring to the table of our relationship from their family, their personality, choices, sins, level of awareness (or lack thereof), emotional or spiritual development, maturity (or lack thereof)—all of this becomes a meal we are subjected to by our spouses. We do the same, offering similar meals to our spouses day in and day out, for decades.

In this chapter, I want to give you some food options you can bring to your spouse. The food we bring to our spouses is our service toward them. What they eat from our lives into theirs is a huge part of our service to our spouses.

It is our responsibility to be aware of the food we are feeding our spouses. We are also responsible for what our food says about the kind of servant we really are toward the one we said we would love, honor, and cherish.

As you read through this chapter, do not come with a heart to measure your spouse's food toward you. If you do, it would mean you still do not get the point of being a servant as opposed to being served. You will be aware of your spouse's food, but you can only change your own food. The good news is, you will only be held accountable for the food you serve to your spouse, not the food they serve to you. So, if you have a food inspector hat tucked away in your closet, you can get it out as long as you are only inspecting the food you serve to your spouse on a daily basis. Remember, servant marriage works to improve us and makes us Christlike, not to be experts in our spouses' weaknesses.

As I am working with a food analogy, I want to take you to a familiar scripture that also utilizes a food analogy to make its point on how we are to live a Christian life. Look at Galatians 5:22-23 (NIV): "But the fruit of the Spirit is love, joy, peace, forbearance, kindness, goodness, faithfulness, gentleness and self-control."

The genesis of this amazing fruit is the Spirit of God, not ourselves. It is true we all have different temperaments, personalities, families of origin, and histories, but each and every one of us, as a believer in Jesus Christ, has access to the Holy Spirit.

This Holy Spirit in us bears identifiable fruit. Through the Spirit, this fruit can flow through us at any time as we allow Him to be expressed in our lives. Being a servant in your marriage is not about trying to produce a better you, but about walking in the Spirit of God, giving *His* fruit to your spouse.

We are the conduits of His Spirit and His fruits toward our spouse. Remember, the conduit does not eat its own fruit. Neither does it benefit from the fruit. The tree does not eat its own fruit; others do. The fruit of the Spirit is to be served to our spouses so they can experience God's fruit in our lives.

I know it might sound ambitious, but we can move toward the goal of giving good fruit or food to our spouse—the kind of fruit that comes from the Spirit and nourishes them. An intentionally well-fed spouse is in better condition than one not fed on a regular basis.

Intentional is a keyword as we move through this process. In my book, *7 Love Agreements*, I highlight this idea. As believers, we can have accidental fruit of the Spirit. You know when you are accidentally patient or kind.

You can actually have intentional fruit of the Spirit as well. You can set goals to allow these fruits to flow through you. You can assess this regularly and even have accountability as you go about releasing fruit toward your spouse.

We will now look more closely at this amazing fruit believers can regularly serve to our spouses if we have the heart and intentionality to do so. Each fruit is different, and will be totally unique to your spouse in how he or she desires or needs it to be fed to him or her.

Love

The first and probably most famous and most needed fruit from which our spouse would benefit is love. Oddly enough, it is usually the first promise we made in our wedding vows before God and all our family and friends as well: to love our spouse.

Love is not a passive emotion. Love is an *in* motion, not an *e*-motion. Love moves toward the other person. "God so loved the world that he gave his one and only Son" (John 3:16, NIV). When God loves, He gives Himself. Love costs us. Christ so loved us that He gave all of Himself at the cross.

Love sometimes has a mushy reputation. True love is all in, all guts, all sacrifice, all cost, no excuses. Love is about being in the game with 100 percent, all of the time. We humans strive to love as well as our God and Savior loves. Love is not for the faint of heart or selfish. The fruit of love will usually be inconvenient and costly for us as we regularly give it to our spouses, day in and day out.

When love is received it can be healing, life-changing, energizing, humbling, touching, and a whole host of other emotions, depending on when it is applied to our hearts. Hopefully you have experienced this. If you have, you would so want your spouse to experience it as well.

Your spouse hungers to be loved—as we all do. According to Gary Chapman in his book, *The 5 Love Languages*, your spouse has a specific way he or she prefers to be loved, whether through touch, praise (words of affirmation), gifts, quality time, or acts of service. What the author does not tell readers is what I have experienced for twenty-five plus years of counseling couples: Your spouse will desire or be wired to be loved in the love language that is hardest for you to give. If your spouse loves touch, you will not want to touch. If he or she likes gifts, you might be prone to be cheap, and so on.

Love is always sacrificial. I am a busy guy with a full counseling practice, and I also write books, speak, make media appearances, and have a busy family. Of course, my spouse would be wired for quality time as the way she receives love.

When we know how our spouse desires to be loved, as a servant, we need to acknowledge this and take responsibility to meet this desire in some consistent manner, without a bad attitude.

Love keeps its heart open in a marriage as we scar each other (not abuse) throughout the journey.

[4] Love is patient, love is kind. It does not envy, it does not boast, it is not proud. [5] It does not dishonor others, it is not self-seeking, it is not easily angered, it keeps no record of wrongs. [6] Love does not delight in evil but rejoices with the truth. [7] It always protects, always trusts, always hopes, always perseveres.

[8] Love never fails.
1 Corinthians 13:4-8, NIV

Over the years of your marriage, you will have ample opportunities to love. As a servant, this is an endless opportunity for you to become even stronger and more loving toward your spouse. In the space below, write out the ways you already know how to love your spouse.

_____
_____
_____

_____

_____

_____

_____

If you were to write out a goal for loving your spouse in an improved manner, what would that goal be?

_____

_____

_____

_____

_____

_____

Joy

As you will recall, as I write this, it is the holiday season. As I get in my truck to go here or there between writing, I turn on the radio and Christmas music fills my otherwise quiet truck. I enjoy hearing "Joy to the World" as I drive around Colorado Springs. Joy is a great fruit of the Spirit. Joy, unlike happiness, has nothing to do with circumstances.

Joy is a disposition in which you or I willfully choose to be grateful, not easily offended, buoyant, upbeat, or optimistic about our lives, our marriages, and pretty much everything. To me, joy is choosing who I am going to be in the story of today and not letting circumstances or people decide who I am going to be.

Joy, like love, is a gift of the Spirit that flows through us to our spouses. Joy is an up type of energy that says, "Life is good," (like the T-shirt). This cheerleader-like energy is contagious and can add a little buoyancy to your spouse. Have you been around a person with real joy? They are stable in a positive position.

The energy of joy really can influence the environment of people around you. If it has been challenging for you to allow joy to flow through you, you might need to focus on this so your spouse gets some of God's fruit of joy in his or her diet from you.

Rate yourself as it relates to the fruit of joy that you give, particularly to your spouse. Give yourself a one for very low and a ten for very high.

Regardless of where you are on the scale, what would it take for you to move one or two numbers up the scale on giving joy to your spouse? In the spaces below, write what it would take for you to move up the scale on the fruit of the Spirit, joy.

1._____

2._____

3._____

Peace

"Peace on the earth, good will to men, let heaven and earth rejoice, let heaven and earth rejoice," could easily have played in my truck this week as well. Like everything else we have been exploring, peace comes from God, not our circumstances.

God is peace. He brings peace to our hearts even when our spouse, children, job, or circumstances may be a little stormy. He is our peace in the midst of a storm. This does not mean we will not get wet, it just means we are more focused on Jesus being in the boat with us rather than on the storm or needing to know how it will turn out.

Peace is trusting the nature and decision of God. I know He is good. Because I know who He is, I can have peace. I might lack knowledge of the circumstances or outcomes, but I do not have to lack knowledge or confidence that He is God. He is in control. He is working things out for my good, even if I do not understand how.

Peace is a fruit that really can give you calmness, faith, and even confidence in God toward your spouse. When in your heart of hearts you have peace, and that nutrition flows out of you, it can truly help calm the storm your spouse is in at any given moment.

There have been countless times when, after Lisa and I prayed about something, we had peace. I know when Lisa is at peace on something. I can sense it.

Peace is a fruit some of us need to practice individually as well as toward our spouse. For some, just meditating on peace for a few weeks can really help soak this fruit into his or her spirit.

How are you on the fruit of peace toward your spouse? Again, from one to ten, rate yourself on the fruit of peace.

Regardless of where you score, what are some things you could do to increase the level of peace you feel and peace you could give to your spouse?

1._____

2._____

3._____

Patience

Well, I do not know about you, but patience is not my strong suit. I find this particular fruit of the Spirit is one that needs regular attention and intention to mature in me.

Have you ever thought of how perfect a marriage situation is to actually grow more patience? God takes two genders from two backgrounds, sprinkles different personalities, preferences, family histories, and giftedness in, and over many decades, forges them to become one flesh.

Wow, the opportunities for patience are endless in a servant marriage. I would wager that even in a healthy marriage of two good Christian people, the opportunity to share small (or not so small) doses of patience would be helpful just about daily. Whether it involves how to best place dishes in the dishwasher, relating to in-laws, agreeing on room temperature, parenting, accepting the way your spouse drives differently, or even just agreeing on how you will be entertained on a given evening—all require patience. Patience is more than tolerance of the differences between you and your spouse. It is more like being gracious and understanding and staying in a servant position during the opportunity to be patient.

I will bet that in some areas, you have become more patient over the years. In the big picture, it is about seeing how amazing your spouse is and accepting their little quirks—the small set of behaviors which may have annoyed you even for decades. This is where God may be working on you to become more lovingly patient before He convicts you of the behavior that bothers you.

Just when you think you have gotten the patience thing down with your spouse, they grow, change, or do a total 180 on you and go to another extreme you also find irritating. No worries on patience, if you need help in that, God will give you children like your spouse to help you gain patience and compassion.

In the space below, write out some areas in which you have already grown mostly patient with your spouse.

1._____

2._____

3._____

4._____

5._____

6._____

7._____

8._____

9._____

10._____

What are some areas in which you could become more patient with your spouse this year?

1._____

2._____

3._____

4._____

How would you go about accomplishing this?

1._____

2._____

3._____

4._____

Who do you know that can help you on your journey to becoming more patient and accountable—to grow in the area of patience?

1._____

2._____

3._____

4._____

Kindness

Kindness is many things. It can be expressed and desired in many different ways, depending on the person. As a studious servant of your spouse, you probably have a pretty good idea what he or she considers an act of kindness toward him or her.

Kindness can be a back rub, foot rub, early morning coffee, picking up the children, putting dishes away, or simply remembering something that is important to your spouse.

Kindness plays ahead of the game. I can think ahead of what is going on in my spouse's day and I can plan to be kind in the way Lisa needs me to be kind that day. Could you imagine living with someone who actually thought ahead of you on a regular basis, anticipating your needs?

I believe most women have this ability fine-tuned when it comes to their children. They can think of what they need for the day, and it is placed in the backpack. Men have this ability fine-tuned at work. They can anticipate what people at the office need from them ahead of time, and they are Johnny-on-the-spot with this.

Kindness toward our spouse is a discipline of letting that fruit of the Spirit flow intentionally and consistently toward our spouse. God already wants to demonstrate kindness toward your awesome spouse. He will even give you ideas to show such kindness to him or her, His child.

In the spaces below, I want you to write out some ways your spouse would receive kindness from you.

1._____

2._____

3._____

4._____

5._____

What are a few goals you could establish if you were intentionally trying to be kind to your spouse?

1._____

2._____

3._____

Goodness

Thank God His Spirit provides the fruit of goodness to flow through us. Goodness is hard to define but clear to see when it is absent. It is kind of like leadership; it is hard to define but clear when someone does not have much of it in his or her life.

Goodness is one of my wife's strongest fruits. She is good to the core. She has no desire to hurt me. When she is being "helpful" (as women tend to be), I never doubt her heart is motivated by goodness. To me, goodness is to have no vile or selfishness motivating me toward you. To me, goodness is a condition of the heart. You either have it or do not have it toward your spouse. If we are self-absorbed and too weak in our character to admit our flaws, we may lack goodness. When goodness is tasted it is so sweet. My experience is that when Lisa has goodness toward me, I really feel loved like it is a privilege to have married someone so pure-hearted.

I do not want you to write this down in a space below, but I do want you to evaluate this fruit of the Spirit on a scale from 1 to 10, with ten being high on goodness. Then where would you generally fall in being good-hearted and unselfish toward your spouse?

In the spaces below, give examples of goodness flowing through you toward your spouse:

1._____

2._____

3._____

4._____

5._____

If you were to improve on goodness toward your spouse, what would your goals be?

1._____

2._____

3._____

Faithfulness

Faithfulness is at the heart of our God. He is a faithful person to us, is He not? He can be depended upon every time. He is faithful to His Word in our lives and is even faithful if we lack faithfulness toward Him.

It is no wonder to me we find faithfulness as a fruit of the Spirit because this is the essence of our God. In my book, *The 7 Love Agreements*, (Strang) I break faithfulness down into several areas:

- Spiritual faithfulness
- Emotional faithfulness
- Sexual faithfulness
- Financial faithfulness
- Parental faithfulness
- Relationship faithfulness

Faithfulness in any area of our lives or marriages means our spouses can depend on us. They can guess how we will act or think because we are faithful to them. My wife can depend on me not to watch pornography or to be inappropriate with women. She knows I will pray with her daily, share my feelings, and hear her feelings daily, and she knows I am not going to spend recklessly, have financial secrets, and I will act like an adult with our children.

Faithfulness gives a sense of relaxation that comes from truth. I can compare it to resting my head on my wife's body. When my weight is fully held by her, my body trusts her and fully relaxes. Faithfulness brings that kind of full relaxation because trust stays consistent.

Of the areas I mentioned on faithfulness, is there any you might need to work on to become a better servant in your marriage?

In the spaces below, write out one or more goals for increasing faithfulness in an area with your spouse:

1._____

2._____

3._____

4._____

Gentleness

I must admit this is probably my second worst area of fruitfulness. I used to call it my personality or "honesty," however; over time I have discovered I am rude, which is the opposite of gentleness. I am naturally direct, which can be helpful in counseling, but not helpful when dealing with Lisa, who is by nature gentle and thoughtful.

Gentle means to be soft, thoughtful, or supportive of another person's soul or circumstances. One time I can absolutely pinpoint I was excellent at this was when I first held Hadassah or Jubal when they were first born. One hundred percent of me was focused on them and their safety. This is what I think of when I think of being gentle. I am fully aware that my strength could be dangerous if I am not consciously thoughtful of the other person.

When it comes to Lisa, when I am making myself more aware of what she is feeling or experiencing than what I am thinking, I am most likely to be gentler with her heart. Gentleness is strength at the service of another's heart or circumstances. When I get this right, I can feel Lisa melt into me.

How about you? How can you allow this fruit of the Spirit of God flow through you? Can you think of a time of the day or circumstances in which your spouse could be helped by being gentle? In the spaces below, list a few of these for yourself:

1._____

2._____

3._____

4._____

If you were to make a couple goals for being gentle with your spouse, what would these goals be?

1._____

2._____

3._____

Self-Control

The Holy Spirit is an excellent author, to say the least. He starts us off on the fruits of the Spirit, which is love. Without truly loving our spouse, it would be challenging to feed them all these fruits on a daily basis. Walking in the Spirit truly goes against our lower nature.

Then He concludes the matter by saying self-control is a fruit of God's Spirit through us, hopefully toward our spouse. I would first need to yield to the Spirit of God if I in any way have any hope to have self-control.

This fruit of the Spirit may have different applications in your personal life's eating smart, exercising, or not over-working. However, in our marriage, how would self-control manifest?

For me, it is about not saying what I am thinking, but regulating my words toward Lisa, considering that she is a daughter of my God. For me, self-control is not lashing out or getting back at someone if I feel they hurt or misunderstood me, but patiently trying to stay calm and resolve an issue.

Self-control involves dying to myself at the time when it is important for me to do so. Even as I have been writing over Christmas week, there have been times when I have been asked to do this or that. I have had to die to what was important to me at that moment to serve Lisa. The self-control part involves *not* spewing out a comment about how important what I was doing was at the moment. Self-control first allows me, in many circumstances, not to say something. This gives me enough time to see a bigger picture, which usually allows me to change how I actually feel or think about something. It lets me appear to be more mature for my precious Lisa.

My experience with self-control, like many of the fruits of the Spirit, has to be intentional to be more fruitful. When I have been more intentional, I have actually seen my heart change and become more open, allowing Him to flow through me, which is much better for everyone.

In the space below, I want you to think of circumstances in which you could grow in the area of self-control.

1._____

2._____

3._____

4._____

Now, take a moment and list how you could be intentional about being self-controlled with your spouse.

1._____

2._____

3._____

I hope you have enjoyed our little journey through the fruits of the Spirit. I know even today I am growing in these areas with Lisa after being married close to thirty years. For you and I, it is a journey to maturity, but this maturation makes us much better servants in our marriage, which glorifies the Father and Father-in-Law tremendously.

"Love is an in motion,
not an e-motion."

The Other Food

I really wish we were all just spiritual beings who filled our spouses with love, joy, and peace twenty-four hours a day. Imagine that level of service after being that consistent on a regular basis. It would be awesome if we were all spiritually consistent athletes.

I am a psychologist, not a philosopher or theologian living in a tower of ideals. Like you, I live in the real world. You know the world I am talking about: alarms early in the morning, running here and there, working, responding to things we do not anticipate, trying to eat or exercise or pray or read, and then trying to get a few minutes to breathe in-between.

I know you can relate. Real life is challenging. I also fully acknowledge we live in a fallen world where sin has affected our souls and bodies. On any given day, our mind, will, or emotions could be impacted or altered by any number of random circumstances, altering the blissful spiritual state we had in our quiet time that morning.

Our bodies are fallen also. Not only do we face potential ailments and physical issues, but simple aging changes as well. I will not even get into the impact of hormones, caffeine, or sugar on our bodies that can totally change the way we think or feel at a given moment.

This kaleidoscope of variables we call the human being can challenge any marriage at any time. You and I are vulnerable to be confused, spiteful, emotionally volatile, willful, and selfish. As humans, we are capable of displaying any number of other undesirable traits.

Unfortunately, our spouses can get a steady diet of what the Scripture calls our "flesh." I like to think of our flesh as the not-so-wonderful parts of us. We all have a flesh, and we are all called to kill it so our spirit man and the fruits of the Spirit can flow through us to our spouses, yet this can be a battle.

In the servant marriage, your flesh will die and you can have a much more fruitful spiritual life in general, and in your marriage. As a servant in your marriage, you will want to be intelligent about your flesh so you can kill it. Your flesh is the enemy in the servant marriage, not your spouse or circumstances. They just expose your heart and whether you are being more fleshly or more spiritual.

I have found that if God is killing an area of my flesh He will keep bringing me the same type of person or circumstances. So if you keep getting upset, angry, or sulk over something, you might do what I had to do and recognize that you could be the problem—not the other person or circumstance. God is using it to expose the flesh in you. If this is happening, it all works out for the good. We eventually get the point, repent, heal, and become better servants to everyone in our lives.

As we walk with our spouse in servant marriage, we want to focus on putting our foot on the gas pedal (so to speak) and walk in the Spirit as we explored in the last chapter. However, many of us also need to put our foot on the brakes of our flesh as well. I want to walk through this from an optimistic viewpoint. Regardless of your flesh, in Christ you can overcome these issues and be a victor in your life.

If we deny or minimize our flesh, we will limit our ability to serve well in our marriage. If we blame others or our spouse, we will be incapable of changing or maturing for God, our spouse, our family, or ourselves. We cannot change that for which we will not take full responsibility!

Let me take a moment and camp on a point that my clients have found helpful as we move toward killing our flesh. So often in our growth we have to move away from blaming others or trying to share responsibility with our spouse for our less-than-wonderful behaviors or beliefs.

Here is what I know for myself and for those I have worked with over the last couple of decades: When I am 100 percent of the problem, I am the solution. When I want to give others responsibility instead of myself, I want them to do the changing for my life to get better.

When I alone am the problem, I can attack the problem at my pace. So as you move toward killing your flesh, look at killing yours, not your spouse's, and take full responsibility.

As you walk through these ideas as we did with the fruits of the Spirit, you will find some things you do not struggle with at all in your flesh. You might also find an area or two you really do struggle with in your flesh, so please read the entire chapter to help you improve. Again, stay focused on your growth, not the growth of your spouse.

Once we know where the battle is inside of us, as servants of the Lord Jesus Christ, we can go to work and kill fleshly stronghold areas. So, be of good cheer. As you go through this, you can come out victorious for the one you love.

We are going to stay in the same book of the Bible we visited in the last chapter on the fruits of the Spirit. Just before this scripture, Paul talks about our flesh or sinful nature. I would like to explore with you the context of this conversation, but before I do, read Galatians 5:16-21 (NIV):

"**16** So I say, walk by the Spirit, and you will not gratify the desires of the flesh. **17** For the flesh desires what is contrary to the Spirit, and the Spirit what is contrary to the flesh.They are in conflict with each other, so that you are not to do whatever[a] you want. **18** But if you are led by the Spirit, you are not under the law.
19 The acts of the flesh are obvious: sexual immorality, im-

purity and debauchery;[20] idolatry and witchcraft; hatred, discord, jealousy, fits of rage, selfish ambition, dissensions, factions [21] and envy; drunkenness, orgies, and the like. I warn you, as I did before, that those who live like this will not inherit the kingdom of God."

Sexuality

As a Christian psychologist, I truly understand why Paul put sexual sins first and last in the list of the products of our flesh. I have been counseling Christian couples for more than twenty-five years. The number one threat to Christian marriages today is pornography, masturbation, social media connection, and sex outside of marriage—in any format. These would all fall under what Paul called "sexual immorality, impurity and debauchery" (Galatians 5:19, NIV).

Sex is a beautiful part of marriage, and I will explore this at length in a future chapter. But here I want to address those who struggle with lust or sexual addiction.

I can give you an idea of just how prevalent this issue is in every church in America. I am often called upon to speak to men about sexual purity in churches of every variety: Catholic, Presbyterian, Methodist, Baptist, non-denominational, interdenominational, and independent. Somewhere in those talks, I will have the men close their eyes and I ask them a question, "How many of you are beyond struggling, and you find that you are addicted to some sexual behavior?" With their eyes still closed, I will ask them raise their hands. Fifty percent or much higher will raise their hands indicating that this is their addiction and struggle. That is a huge percentage. If you are a woman, you have a fifty percent chance or greater that your husband secretly struggles with a sexual addiction.

I strongly encourage women everywhere to ask their husbands about the last time they masturbated or used pornography. I also encourage them to check the history file on their computers, iPads, and cell phones to see what is truly going on. I cannot tell you how many women have called our office after they or one of their children accidentally discovered dad's porn viewing, chatting, or emails to other women or men for romantic or sexual hookups.

We live in the most easily accessible and perverted sexual culture in world history. Having accountability software is helpful, and occasionally asking or checking up is helpful. You definitely want to catch this behavior as soon as possible.

This, however, is not only a guy problem anymore. Although some Christian women will look at porn, it is not the situation I see in my office very often. Usually, she is on Facebook or some other form of social media and connects with an old boyfriend or starts getting attention or praise from a stranger online. They chat and over time she agrees to meet. Romantic and sexual behavior then follows. Countless couples I have counseled have suffered damage to their relationships due to the Internet and social media. The best practice is to keep all social media mutual when married.

If your sexuality is trapped instead of free, this will limit you greatly in your marriage. Keeping a secret is deadly. This is why it is so important to be honest with each other in this area of your marriage. Sex addiction robs you of spiritual, emotional, and moral maturity. It leaves a man acting and reasoning as an adolescent, and unable to spiritually lead his household.

I will never forget a woman in Canada who came up to me at a conference where I was speaking. She came up after the service and said, "Dr. Weiss, my husband just won't be the spiritual leader of our home." I told her what I tell women all the time: "Go home and ask him how often he is masturbating or looking at pornography."

She brought him back the next night and, sure enough, he had a huge secret porn and self-sex life she did not know about. He started in a group and they were able to start on the road to him becoming spiritually, emotionally, and morally mature as he became free from sexual addiction.

If you have this issue, I want to encourage you. I have been free from sexual addiction for more than twenty-eight years, verifiable through polygraphs. Anyone who is willing to do the work of recovery can get and stay free their entire life.

As a servant in your marriage, if you struggle with sexual secrets, whether it includes sexual abuse or addiction, I highly recommend you take full responsibility to heal so you can be a better servant of the Lord and to your spouse.

I am going to quickly list some books/DVDs that can be very helpful if you are the sex addict, spouse of a sex addict, or someone struggling with lust or sexual impurity. These are available on our website. We also have a free app that offers tips for men who struggle, tips for their spouse, tips for their marriage every day of the year. Go to your app store and download "Dr. Dougs Tips." Here are some books that can be helpful (for descriptions, go to http://www.drdougweiss.com):

- *Lust-Free Living*
- *The Final Freedom*
- *101 Freedom Exercises*
- *Steps to Freedom*
- *Helping Her Heal*
- *Partners: Healing From His Addiction*
- *Partners Recovery Guide*
- *Beyond Love*

I included materials for the wife of a sex addict called *Partners* because sex addiction in any form impacts the wife. Her pain is real. So are her feelings of betrayal, disgust, fear, and concern about the future of her husband's choices. She can and often will need a journey toward healing as well.

If you need more help, you can schedule a phone session with a therapist who has been trained by me. You can also schedule a three or five day intensive with me at my Colorado Springs office. This can be a boot camp for you and your marriage and a walk toward freedom, if it has been an issue for you.

Now, I want to talk about the opposite side of sexual lust. We call this intimacy anorexia. This can also be a very strong flesh pattern that deeply affects the marriage. I will be brief here, but if this is an issue, get materials on this or schedule an intensive.

The sexual addict is married to the lust or the pleasure of acting out. The intimacy anorexic is married to themselves, withholding love from their spouse, leaving them feeling married and alone. Intimacy anorexia is the active withholding of spiritual, emotional, and sexual intimacy. The characteristics of intimacy anorexia are:

- Being too busy for one's spouse
- Ungrounded blaming
- Withholding love
- Withholding praise
- Withholding sex
- Withholding spiritually
- Withholding feelings
- Undue criticism
- Controlling with anger/silence
- Controlling money

If you or your spouse has intimacy anorexia, this will really hinder you from being a loving servant to your spouse. The blame, criticism, or aloneness over the years is extremely painful. Below is a list of materials that can be helpful for intimacy anorexia.

- *Intimacy Anorexia* (Book/DVD)
- *Intimacy Anorexia Workbook*

- *Intimacy Anorexia Steps*
- *Married and Alone* (Book/DVD)
- *Married and Alone Workbook*
- *Married and Alone Steps*

If you need more help with this, you can always call for a telephone counseling appointment or a three or five day intensive in Colorado Springs.

Sexual flesh strongholds can be a huge impairment to having a great servant marriage. I have seen so many couples heal from sexual addiction or intimacy anorexia that I can truly say, if a person is willing to do the work, they can heal and have a better more mature marriage than they ever thought possible.

However, refusing to heal in either of these two areas intentionally condemns your spouse to a marriage that will have more pain and suffering than the Lord designed for him or her. Remember your Father-in-Law God wants you to be the best servant in your marriage. If that means addressing these issues, I would. I believe it would put a big smile on His face to see you heal these areas so you can be an awesome spouse.

Idolatry

In the old Bible days, you and I know that idolatry was literal. People, even believers, sometimes had idols they worshipped. Idolatry can have a couple of meanings today.

The first type of idol is believing or behaving as if things or objects have more value than people or God. For instance, when you place the value of a new toy, car, dress, or any object, above others and give it value to make you feel different, more valuable, or better than others, it can be an idol. You have given a thing a power that God has not given it. It is totally fine to have cars, houses, jewelry, or even the best toy ever, as long as God is first and it is not an idol.

The second type of idol is what Ezekiel 14 talks about. We can put idols in our hearts. We can worship ourselves, others, or secular or ungodly ideas, and these can become idols in our lives.

You can tell when you have an ideology or belief that is an idol when Scripture frustrates you in the area of that ideology or belief. If someone confronts you on this in love and you are offended, this can be a sign that you have an idol in your heart. Some may have possibly been offended after reading some of the pages in this book about God as king in our marriage.

Ideas, entitlement, and ego can all become idols in our current context. If idols stay in our heart we will tend to value an ideology over the value of a person. Being right instead of being loving might be an example of a person's idol. Pride can be an idol, for example. If we cannot say we are wrong, the overvaluing of self could be self-idolatry instead of humility.

In a servant marriage, if we have idolatry like materialism or huge financial debt, we need to look at this as evidence we may well value things over people—especially our spouse and family. If you feel this is an area that needs to be addressed, talk together and be in agreement on how you can resolve these issues.

You deserve an awesome servant marriage. Christ died so we could enjoy our spouse our entire life. Idolatry limits our life in so many ways, including our marriage. If you walk in areas of idolatry, you can tend to devalue your spouse or truth. This can be annoying or damaging, depending on where the idols lie, so allow God to address any issue of external or internal idolatry so you can enjoy a much fuller servant marriage.

Witchcraft

This one is rarely a problem in a contemporary Christian marriage. I have never heard of anyone chanting spells or witchcraft type curses over their spouse. That said, we need to look at the core thought of witchcraft.

The core idea is, *I can make someone do something or have something done to him or her without his or her involvement*. In other words, *I can impose my will on my spouse without him or her knowing, giving consent, or agreeing*. Some examples of witchcraft are: manipulating through anger, withholding sex or money or knowledge about certain things, and many more.

The idea here is manipulation. Manipulation is not healthy for a servant of the Lord. We do not have to get our way; we can learn and negotiate with our spouses.

We do not have to bully each other with anger, threats, money, sex, or silence to manipulate our spouses. By practicing any of this, we are trying to get our way much like someone in witchcraft might. The short version of this witchcraft idea is one of imposing our will on someone without consent.

As servants, we should be far away from manipulating our spouses. However, some of us have learned that manipulation, lying, and withholding information or affection can move the outcome in our favor. If this is part of your flesh, you want to target an area or two at a time and get accountable with someone of the same gender so you can heal and become an awesome servant of the Lord.

Hatred

Hatred is a tricky flesh pattern. Hatred is not the absence of love, but often a love that is hurt or wounded. Hatred is not the opposite of love; indifference is the opposite of love. Hatred is not the absence of love, it is the absence of value. It is not that I do not love you, it is that I do not value you.

Once you turn an infinite soul created in God's image into a thing, object, or "it," you devalue it so completely that you can justify manifesting your hate any way you want to: anger, control, blame, label, pathologize, withhold sex, withhold money, curse, or shame.

Hatred devalues your spouse, denies them your value and respect, and then decimates him or her at will. Hatred is like a video game. It makes your spouse not real as a person, making it easy for you to mistreat or disregard him or her at will. In regard to intimacy anorexics; they can be prone to this behavior, though others are capable of it as well.

As servants of the Lord Jesus Christ, we may feel strong feelings—even hate—but it would be a sin to manifest hatred toward our spouse. This loss of value is despicable and unacceptable for a Christian. We are responsible for how well we treat others, especially our spouses, 100 percent of the time.

If you find yourself devaluing your spouse, seek help. It may be you were someone's object (not a soul) of contempt and you are now perpetrating this. Hatred may be a way for you to control or manipulate, which puts you back into witchcraft.

If you struggle here, do not keep it a secret. Go to your pastor or counselor and discuss the hatred issue. You deserve freedom to see your spouse as an amazing creature even if you are not happy with him or her at a given moment.

Discord

Discord has more to do with the way we communicate. All of us are probably guilty of a curt or hurtful word on a rare occasion, but we ask forgiveness and move on. This is not discord.

Scripturally, discord is an ongoing pattern of battling, tri-angulating behaviors, or creating communication styles that do not solve a problem. Conflict is a beautiful part of life; it causes growth, change, and can often give us a better life. How we go through conflict is all-important. Remember, the God who made us is the Father-in-Law God who is present during these conflicts, as He is om-nipresent.

If conflict is about winning, you both have already lost and discord will be present. This format of arguing is usually emotional bullying or blackmailing, but will not solve the problem. If you are moving to several topics or bringing up the past to neutralize your spouse, this may be discord, if it is practiced regularly. Shaming would be another form of discord when used regularly. When we shame our spouse, we declare that we are controlling, angry, wounded, sick, and unhealthy. This is one person declaring a reality to the other and demanding it be ad-hered to for the comfort of the perpetrator. This would be discord.

As you can see, you can create an endless number of communication systems that could create and maintain discord. If you are creative, you could change systems but maintain discord.

In my book, *The Ten Minute Marriage Principle*, I outline a simple process I call "fighting fair." If you would like the handout version of this, send me an email. The points are simple:

1. Identify only one problem.
2. Separately write down your feelings about the problem.
3. Separately write down several options for solving the problem.
4. Combine all of your options.
5. Vote 1-10 as to how much you like each solution separately (10 being you like the idea a lot).
6. Consider the solution with the highest combined score to be the winning solution.

There are many conflict resolution strategies written by so many people. If this is an area you struggle with individually or as a couple, you will want to be creative and very good at resolving conflict. As a servant, you can create options to solve issues as smoothly as possible.

Serving during conflict is probably one of the hardest tests for us as we serve our spouses. In our flesh, we want to be understood rather than be understanding. We would rather be heard than hear. We might strive to be right or win rather than humble, honest, and open-minded. As a servant toward our spouse, the best practice is to focus on healing and creating solutions. This allows us to keep the value of our spouse as a person higher than the value of the immediate conflict.

Knowing how to resolve conflict versus merely fighting is critical to avoid creating cracks in our marriage or building resentment in our hearts. Regardless of the method, formula, or structure you use or create to solve problems, it is important that you both stay valued within the process of resolution.

Fractions

This is similar to discord. The way I separate discord from fractions is, in fractions, one or both spouses involve or bring others into the conversation, even hypothetically. This could be as simple as quoting others to build your campaign/argument against your spouse. You or your spouse might literally involve a third, fourth, or fifth person, whether family, friends, in-laws, or pastors. Again, this is one person building up their cause or campaign against the other one.

Do you notice the similarities of both of these processes? They are against the spouse; their enemy is the spouse, not the problem or issue at hand. As a servant, if you do better or as good as you can on understanding your spouse (per the previous chapter) you could probably defuse creating fractions.

I find it fascinating that Paul took this particular approach of discord and separated it out. When you need to involve others, it is best if the purpose of getting together is to understand each other or the issues in order to solve the problem. If this is your particular flesh area, to end this pattern in your life and marriage, it is probably best that you work on it with someone of the same gender.

As a couple, from time to time, you might be at a legitimate impasse on a big issue. We all need wisdom at times in our marriage. Agreeing on whom to seek for counsel is important. When doing this, again, the goal is for better understanding and creating solutions. This would be the opposite of creating fractions because the goal would be to walk in unity on a subject or decision.

Envy

With envy, the short of it is you want something someone else has: a characteristic, strength, gifts, circumstances, money, ministry, possessions, or more. I think envy is why God, in the tenth commandment, tells us not to lust after anything of our neighbors.

The problem with envy is, it causes its victim to be unhappy or resentful at the current blessings and station in life that either God or choices have dictated. In general, envy can corrupt a soul and make us entirely ungrateful, even bitter in good circumstances.

In a marriage, envy creeps in especially around the early childbearing years. The wife might resent her body changes, while her husband does not. She may not work and resent that, or she may have to go back to work and resent that. He could resent or envy her if she works or if she does not work.

In the other form of envy, you want your spouse to have characteristics you find desirable in another person. You might wish he or she were more fun, rich, intellectual, sexual, organized, spiritual, or many other things. Envy can create an entire list of things for you to resent—all things your spouse is not. Be careful of this type of envy. It makes you focus on what you do not have instead of what you do have. The obvious cure, of course, is to focus on being grateful for the characteristics your spouse has that are a blessing to you.

Envy is usually sneaky and slow as it moves in a marriage. An easy way to know if you have envy is to look for the feeling of resentment toward your spouse. If you struggle with this, try talking to a wise friend, a clergyperson, or counselor. Sometimes hurt is a precursor to envy, so you might need someone to help you process what is going on with you.

Drunkenness

Earlier we explored sexual addiction and out of control sexual behaviors. Drunkenness is alcohol usage in excess. Most Christians do not struggle with drinking alcohol in excess, though some do.

However, as a counselor who works with Christian couples, I have seen excess in gluttony, spending, debt, prescription drugs, anger, and many other behaviors. Out of control behaviors hurt everyone. Sadly, the spouse with these behaviors is usually in denial as to how he or she uses something or someone to medicate his or her life.

Addictions or out of control behaviors can be addressed and healed using my series called *Recovery for Everyone*; a book, exercise workbook, twelve step workbook, and DVD set. Anyone can walk out of the grip of out of control behaviors.

If you have out of control behavior, it limits your maturity and impacts your marriage immensely. As a servant, you will want to get support and walk out of this limiting behavior so you can have an awesome life and marriage.

So, how did you survive this rugged journey through the terrain of our flesh? Most of us have something to think about growing through or actually get aggressive about moving past. Again, in Christ there is not only hope, but strength, and practical applications you can make to have a servant marriage.

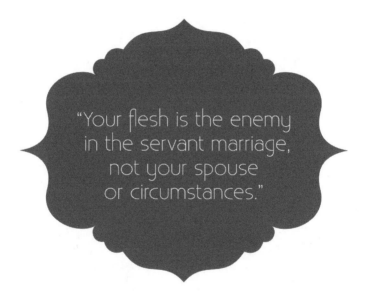

"Your flesh is the enemy
in the servant marriage,
not your spouse
or circumstances."

Grief

As a counselor, I have helped many people grieve many different events or realities in their lives. In grief counseling, the model for grief comes from Kübler Ross who studied people dying. She identified the grief stage as: shock, denial, anger, bargaining, sadness, and acceptance.

The very first stage of grief is shock. Shock is kind of visceral feeling throughout one's body. When you genuinely hold tightly to an idea and a truth comes against that idea, you can experience shock. It can feel like disconnection or pain or numbness depending on the intensity of what you are grieving.

The next stage is denial. This is a challenging stage. Some people, even after hearing a truth, can stay in denial about it indefinitely. At the core of you, you are aware that something is true but you keep pushing against it because it might cost you to change, grow, or admit you were wrong. Sadly, usually the last person to know they are in denial is the person in denial.

Anger is the next stage of grief. I find that people who are losing something can get angry, be it power, control, money, or just their emotional footing as they integrate a new idea. Sometimes these people get angry when I say something at a conference like, "Pornography is biblically unacceptable." As they grieve the loss of this medication in their life and stop using it, they not only agree with the message but the messenger as well.

Bargaining is a challenging stage of grief. It wants you to just make the pain go away. Bargaining basically says, "If this had not happened, then that would not have happened," or "If this is not true, then that is not true." Bargaining is another stage that can go on for years. The soul is still trying to process the pain of a significant loss.

Bargaining can look like blame or obsession over a detail of what occurred. For example, a man who has an accident might say that if the roads had not been so wet he would have avoided the accident, when in fact, he was driving under the influence of alcohol. Some people pick up causes in their bargain stage, which is also a way to process the loss of someone or something.

Sadness is the next to last stage of grief. You just feel down about the reality you are grieving. This stage is less about fighting grief and more about moving you into acknowledging the new reality.

Acceptance is the final stage of grief. Getting to acceptance is sometimes a very long process. Depending on the painfulness of the reality or the resistance of the person to accept the reality, acceptance may be a short or long process.

Why am I talking about grief? As I teach the ideas in the next chapters, accepting your role as a servant can go against your current beliefs culturally and emotionally. Years of wrong behaviors or beliefs might well be challenged in you as you 100 percent accept your role as the servant of your spouse.

I find that those with strong entitlement dispositions, and men from cultures that promote that men being served tend to grieve the hardest. The denial that they are to serve can go on indefinitely, keeping them stuck and more self-serving than is healthy. The fact that I would even suggest that they are called by God to serve someone else can really get some men and women very angry. Some resist service because of abuse or having poor boundaries in the past, so anger can arise there as well.

Bargaining can include, "I'll serve when they start serving me." One could feel sadness that life as one once knew it could be over.

Acceptance is a mixed bag. Some accept their role in marriage as a servant with an attitude of "I have to." This type of acceptance makes every opportunity to serve a building of resentment for their calling. Those who accept their role as a servant with an "I get to" attitude see opportunities to serve their spouse without a whole lot of effort and resentment.

Serving is our spiritual bodybuilding. Marriage is our gym, and our home and family provide the workout. For decades they build us stronger to become more patient, kind, loving, less able to be offended, more forgiving, and I might say, just better believers in Jesus Christ.

Serving is not a chore; it is a lifestyle of freedom. I am not talking about being abused by a tyrant, whether male or female. If that is occurring in your marriage, talk to your pastor or counselor and serve your spouse by getting him or her the help he or she needs!

Every tyrant I have met is like a bully in a schoolyard. They are abuse victims who are afraid of intimacy, have addictions or secrets, or just cannot be authentic, so they reject themselves and control others to limit being known or hurt.

I would not want any man or woman to be taken advantage of or abused. This teaching is to serve by choice, not by command or due to control. Our service comes from love, not fear. I volunteer daily to serve Lisa and my family. Honestly, some days I am better at it than others. Just as in any sport, you have awesome days and less-than-awesome days.

I encourage you to read through the following chapters and hear what I believe God has shown me to help all of our marriages to become supernatural places to live. When the heart of a servant beats in you and you are led by the Holy Spirit, marriage can be fun and enjoyable.

Take today for example. I flew in to speak at a conference last night at 11 p.m., so did not get to bed until around 12:30 a.m. I had to present our intimacy marriage conference at 8:15 a.m. I had to eat a quick breakfast before teaching several hours that day. During lunch, I checked my phone and saw I had received a very nice text from my bride. That little act of service made my day. The fact that she considered my circumstances meant a lot to me.

Imagine a marriage where each person considers the other person's day, their heart, and their needs on a consistent basis. That would feel pretty good, would it not?

This reminds me of an old preacher's story:

A man dies and he meets St. Peter at the pearly gates. Peter says, "Before I take you to your final destination, let me show you heaven and hell." So Peter takes the man to heaven.

The man sees a huge banquet table that goes on for an endless number of miles. On the table is an abundant amount of food. He observes that everyone in heaven is healthy, plump, and happy. However, he notices forks are attached to their upper forearms. Then Peter takes him to hell. Interestingly, the man sees exactly the same banquet table filled with lavish amounts of food. And again, people have forks attached to their upper forearms. However, the people in hell are not plump or healthy; they are emaciated, almost like skeletons. The man says to Peter, "I don't get it. Why are the people so different in heaven and hell? It looks like the same setup to me?"

"In hell," Peter replies, *"they are trying to feed themselves and the forks won't let them pick up the food and get it to their mouths. In heaven, they learned how to feed each other.*

The moral of the story is quite simple. If we focus only on ourselves and serving ourselves, we grow weaker and weaker spiritually, for sure. However, if we are focused on feeding our spouses and they are focused on serving us, we both stay healthier, happier, and may even be more spiritually plump.

The servant marriage awaits all of us willing to take the journey step by step, day by day with an awesome person (our spouse). Who knows? You might just have some heavenly moments here on earth.

"Serving is not a chore;
it is a lifestyle of freedom."

Understanding

I want to take you into my world for a moment. To be specific, it is Monday morning in my office. It does not matter what Monday, because every Monday for the last fifteen years or so I have been doing marriage intensives that start on Monday.

A marriage intensive is when a couple flies into Colorado Springs to spend three to five days in intensive counseling with myself or a counselor who has been trained by me. They do individual counseling, couples counseling, go to groups, watch DVDs, and complete homework daily.

Many of these couples have tried counseling before and failed. Some couples just want to improve their marriage after there has been pornography and/or sexual addiction, infidelity and/or intimacy anorexia. (Intimacy anorexia is the active withholding of spiritual, emotional or sexual intimacy from one's spouse.)

Back to Monday morning. I greet my clients, have a brief discussion, and then quickly get information as to why they are here. The couples then often explain the addiction, intimacy anorexia, or other challenging issues they face and want to move past in order to feel like lovers and friends again.

Typically, not long into stating their goals, they begin to disagree. Often it is very clear to me that the husband and wife do not understand one another. As a psychologist, I know the couple will not do well reaching the goals they came to achieve unless they understand each other.

The same is true of any marriage, regardless of where it is on the continuum of marital happiness. If a husband and wife are unable to understand each other, they will have significantly greater challenges, conflicts, escalated conversations, and unmet needs in their marriage.

In a servant marriage it is very important that both husband and wife have the skill of really understanding each other. How can you truly serve someone if you cannot understand him or her? That would be challenging, to say the least. However, if you were given a skill to help you consistently understand each other year after year, decade after decade, you could be a better servant toward your spouse. I want to help you develop this skill so you can be an awesome servant to your spouse and practice growing in your understanding of him or her all the days of your life, till death do you part.

To begin this training, the first thing you need is a clear definition of the word, "understanding." I am not going to clutter your mind or heart with numerous dictionary definitions of the word, or tell you the Greek or Hebrew word for it. Though I am able to do this, I am so pragmatic that my experience is, you would find something your spouse is not doing in one of those definitions and attempt to get him or her to do that one aspect of understanding better. You would believe that by fixing that one thing you will have solved the difficulties in your marriage. (I am human as well and could be tempted to do the same.)

To avoid any mental gymnastics, I am going to state a very simple definition of understanding, and then give you a simple way to experience whether or not *you* truly understand the definition.

Understanding: "to stand under"

What I love about this definition over several academic versions of this word is that 100 percent of the focus is on where you are in the process, not where your spouse is in the process.

The next step in developing this skill is to discover how well you stand under your spouse to understand him or her. You have heard the saying, "It is better to understand than to be understood." There is real truth to that. As I understand Lisa, I get revelations of who she is and her heart, which help me adapt and serve her better. If you and I grow in the skill of understanding, we open up all kinds of opportunities to have a great servant marriage.

I want you to do something very simple. Follow these instructions after reading them:
1) Put the book down.
2) Point the fingers on your left hand down and into the palm of your right hand as illustrated below.
3) Totally relax your left hand until you feel the total weight of your left hand on the palm of your right hand.

Illustration:

When you actually feel the full weight of your left hand, your right hand is "standing under," or understanding.

When you do this simple exercise you can physically feel when the left hand lets go of the weight and the right hand holds the weight. When the right hand truly holds the weight of the left hand, the right hand is <u>understanding</u>.

I see this same reality in my office when a woman or man feels misunderstood and escalates to be understood. After following the understanding protocol, the misunderstood spouse de-escalates and relaxes and melts just like your left hand does when the right hand stands under the left hand. It is possible to de-escalate your spouse (though not always, if they have a mental illness).

Before we start, let me give you some examples of mistakes couples make in attempting to understand each other.

Bob: "I was really disappointed when the neighbor didn't thank me for shoveling their driveway."

Sue: "You don't need to be thanked. That's not why you did it, I hope. Can you help me with the dishes?"

Tom: "I'm really tired. It was a long day at the office and the Johnson's music lesson went long."

Sharon: "You think you're tired. I cleaned house, did laundry, made dinner, and put two of the four kids to bed."

Alice: "I really want to talk to you about our interaction this morning. I really felt put down."

Hank: "No thank you. You were wrong then and you're still wrong."

Barb: "I am really feeling overwhelmed with the kids, school, and working full time."

John: "Get up an hour earlier. That should help. Who's picking up Lacey at dance tonight?"

Hopefully you have never been a part of such interactions with your spouse. Sadly, most of us—me included—have had less-than-wonderful moments in communication with our spouse. Take a quick look at these errors in understanding.

When Bob was talking to Sue about being disappointed, Sue ran right over his feelings. Bob actually could have felt put-down because of Sue's lack of understanding. Although feelings are not truth, they are real; and Sue missed an opportunity to understand Bob.

Sharon made a very classic mistake with Tom. She made it all about her; her pain, challenges, and difficulties. Tom was not only unheard and not validated, he was inserted into a competition he could not ever win. Making it about us instead of our spouses is a very common mistake in understanding.

Hank made another classic mistake with Alice. That mistake is blaming, and of course, not even being willing to talk about the issue. Blaming and stonewalling one's spouse is an absolute way to create distance instead of closeness and understanding.

John made probably the most classic mistake in the

world. Instead of understanding his wife, he solved her problem. If Barb is going to school, working, and being a mom, she probably knows how to solve problems. She wanted to be understood by John. She wanted John to stand under her.

Now that we have seen some classic mistakes others have made, we can smile and see that there definitely is a better way to serve our spouse—by understanding them.

Understanding

The skill of standing under your spouse has six distinct steps. Each step is in sequence. You do not want to skip steps in this process. This process is way shorter than arguing and can move you toward a place where you can actually solve problems.

Before we go into the skill of understanding, I need to take a moment and give a few quick points on gender and conversation.

First, I want to address the married man reader. Your wife truly desires to be understood. When she is understood consistently, she will be less stormy, moody, and angry, and she will operate more at her full potential. Also, there is no shortcut or short way to understanding your spouse. It takes time, effort, focus, and more patience than you usually have, and it will almost always be inconvenient. However, I have *never* met a man who *practiced this exercise* with his wife who was not grateful for it when he needed it.

Now I want to address the married woman reader. Your husband is a man and must practice understanding to get good at it, similarly he would need to practice to get good at football or fixing cars. Do not believe that just because you are a woman, you do not create pain in your husband's life. We all sin and create pain in relationships. Finally, your husband needs to be understood and validated at a heart level as well. When he is understood, he will function optimally and become happier in the marriage. He also will do better if you ask to be understood before you get into a conversation where you need to just be understood. He will not intuitively get this right all the time. If you say, "John, I would like you to use the understanding tool in this conversation," he will know what you expect of him.

1. Hearing Their Heart

Listening to someone's heart goes beyond listening to the words he or she is saying. It is likely you have had that experience in which someone repeated almost word for word what you said, but it was clear they had not listened carefully or comprehended what you said. Hearing someone's heart is more than data collection. The information is only one aspect of hearing someone. Hearing someone when they want to be understood is different than just pushing data back and forth.

First, the person desiring to be understood is usually experiencing a challenge with emotion, discomfort, or pain which is causing them to desire it. This desire to be understood automatically puts the communication at a different point than just general conversation. You can tell when you hit this point with someone because he or she will typically amplify this through intensity and/or repetition to get you to switch into the gear of understanding.

To hear someone's heart is to hear who he or she *is* during the communication as well as what he or she is saying. The person is communicating words, ideas, histories, humor (or lack of it), sarcasm, emotion, or motives, all with various levels of frequency and intensity.
To communicate with another human being and genuinely hear his or her heart requires significant intentionality on your part. Remember, when someone desires understanding, you must be fully present until you feel his or her weight. This is not a time to check a cell phone message, text someone, watch TV, or sing along with the radio.

This being desires to be understood, and if this desire is not met with skill and focus, communication could escalate into one of those "How did we get here?" conversations that can last for hours or days.

Hearing your spouses' heart allows him or her to be heard first, without judgment, interruption, solution, or change of topic. If you feel you are present and hearing all about them without drifting into thinking about you or talking about you—no other channels are operating— you are probably hearing your spouse's heart.

2. Feelings

Emotions are a very tricky part of the understanding process. I will illustrate this lack of understanding for you in regard to emotions and feelings. When I went to Bible college, they did not teach me about feelings. Even after I graduated from seminary with two degrees, one in divinity and one in marriage and family counseling, they did not teach me about feelings. As I earned my doctorate in psychology, I was still not taught to identify or communicate feelings.

Nowhere in our Western culture are we trained to share feelings, except perhaps in therapy. Yet we all need to be able to identify and communicate feelings.

Before I go into the skill aspect, let me remind you of a few salient points about feelings. Most of us have no training in identifying or communicating our feelings or hearing the feelings of others. Emotions or feelings are *not* thoughts about something or someone, but rather how someone feels. Feelings are *not* facts or truth. You can feel fat and factually not be overweight. When you are in an emotional reality, it is separate from anything else. You are feeling what you are feeling—that is it. The feeling is not moral, right, or wrong; it is just what you are feeling at the time.

This second step on feeling is where most people drop the ball (especially men, but not exclusively). The spouse who desires to be understood will not be understood if the other spouse tries to put that spouse's feelings into a logical or moral formula. This will only frustrate the spouse who desires to be understood, and he or she might escalate.

Rather than avoid the messy, unpredictable world of feelings, I want you to go into this world with your spouse and—like a GPS—find exactly where your spouse is, emotionally. Practically, this works by asking him or her: "How did that cause you to feel?" or, "What were you feeling?" Once you get a feeling word (alone, excited, calm, demeaned, or other), ask for more: "What else did you feel?" "Where else have you felt that feeling?" "When was the first time you felt that feeling?"

A word of caution here: Do not be duped when you ask for what they are feeling and they start making complete sentences, go on with the story, or do not tell you a feeling. Gently ask: "Before you continue; I was wondering what you were feeling," or, "That sounds like a thought, honey, but what were/are you feeling?" *Do not* ask for more feelings if you did not get the first one to start.

Here are some examples:

Mark: "Unbelievable! I can't believe it! The guys knew all along. I've got to be the stupidest guy on the planet."

Stacy: "What's going on? What are you talking about?"

Mark: "The guys at the office led me to believe that my supervisor wanted a presentation on a new direction for our business development. I worked on it for weeks.

They knew this wasn't the right direction, but they hung me out to dry. I looked like a fool when my boss asked me how long I had been working on it."

Stacy: "How did you feel?"

Mark: "What do you mean? These guys had it in for me! They saw me climbing and took me down a notch."

Stacy: "That sounds painful . . . but what is your best guess at how you felt?"

Mark: "Betrayed. Stupid. Humiliated. Really duped."

Stacy: "Any other feelings?"

Mark: "Nope. I think that's it . . . other than feeling totally foolish."

Mark would have stayed in his head not his heart. His heart needed some understanding. Had Stacy not gone on and asked Mark for what he was feeling, it could have taken days for him to identify feeling betrayed, stupid, humiliated, or foolish.

I realize that asking your spouse what he or she is feeling can be messy. However, as their servant, taking this step in the understanding process is huge. This bravery amplifies when the issue they desire to discuss is you or something you did. However, even if they desire to be understood by you or something you did or did not do, be brave and ask them what they are feeling.

Before I go on to the next step, I have to say I under-stand that talking about feelings might be challenging for some. If this is you, I highly recommend my book, *Emotional Fitness* (see Appendix). As a servant toward your spouse, the more emotionally fit you are, the better your service will be toward them.

This book is very pragmatic in providing exercises any-one can use to advance to a much higher level of skill to identify, communicate, feel feelings, and even master changing their feelings, no matter how emotionally illit-erate or shut down he or she may be. I would even say this emotional fitness manual could fill in quite a gap in most of our development emotionally. I have used these skills with my clients and in sixty days, observed their emotional abilities grew significantly.

3. Validating

Validating is the very core of the understanding process. This is when your spouse feels inside that you have ac-tually heard him or her. This stage is the point in the process when your spouse feels you are holding his or her weight.

Remember to stay on course. The target is to hear them and not to argue, get your point across, be understood yourself, or explain yourself. Understand, it is all about him or her at that moment; not you. This is a process and a skill, and once you have mastered it, you can serve with it the rest of your life.

Validating is *not* agreeing with your spouse that their reality or feelings are truth. You are just validating that what they are feeling is what they are feeling at the moment.

Validating your spouse can be done in statements such as:
"I can see you're really feeling _____ (feelings they already mentioned)"

"I could easily feel _____ (same feelings) if that happened to me."
"Of course, you're feeling _____ (same feelings). That is totally understandable in those circumstances."

Validating is simply saying, "This is where you are," or, "I see you." Validating is essential for your spouse (or anyone) to be understood. Validating says, "You're valuable," and, "Where you are right now is permissible" without judgment and with some empathy for where he or she is at the moment. My experience with clients—male or female—is that when they are validated there is no escalation, and calmness enters them and their relationship.

We will now continue with Stacy and Mark. She already knows his feelings, so now she wants to move toward Mark and validate his feelings.

Stacy: "Of course you felt betrayed. It looks like you were. I understand how you would feel humiliated before your coworkers when your boss asked how much time you had spent on that presentation. I would have felt duped and stupid, had that happened to me today."

Notice Stacy stays where Mark is. She does not offer advice, tell Mark how awful her day was, or tell him to suck it up and help her with dinner. To understand is to stay with the person where they are. This takes just moments, but it can save hours of misunderstanding.

4. Take Responsibility

This step is only needed if you were the one causing the issue, challenge, or pain. If you have difficulty saying you are wrong, make mistakes, struggle with pride, or have intimacy anorexia, this part of the understanding process can be very difficult.

If you caused all or some of the pain or issue at hand, you will want to take full responsibility for your part. Here are some example statements: "I can see the pain (or feelings) you're having and I caused that/them," or, "I am responsible for this issue and responsible for the pain or feelings you are having right now," or, "Since I caused this issue, I am fully responsible for what occurs; even the feelings you are currently expressing toward me," and, "I'm wrong here, clearly see it, and I want to take responsibility not only for the issue, but for how you're feeling about your _____ (feelings or pain)."

In the example of Mark and Stacy, Stacy did not cause, nor is in any way responsible for what happened to Mark. Therefore, Stacy would not do step four (this one) in this process. She would go right to step five. However, here is another example to illustrate this step:

Charlie and Linda have had a long-standing issue throughout their seven years of marriage. Whenever they go to Charlie's parents, he reverts to being a child and lets his mother say anything she wants about Linda. They have talked about this several times, but Charlie fails at intervening more than he succeeds. We will go through this step by step through step four where Charlie takes full responsibility.

Linda: "I can't believe you did it again. I can't believe you let your mother go off on me about how I don't let our children drink sodas. You and I agree this is best for their health, short and long term, and you just let her go at me and blame me for how different our kids are going to be and how they won't have friends."

Charlie (using the understanding process): "Linda, I have no defense for how I acted. We talked about this before and how you need me to protect you at my parent's house. I hear that you experienced me letting her go off on you. What were you feeling then and now (step 2)?"

Linda: "I felt abandoned. I've told you that before. I felt torn trying to honor her and yet have my own beliefs. I felt challenged and belittled."

Charlie: "What else (step 3)?"

Linda: "I just feel so alone when this happens again and again."

Charlie: "I am fully responsible for not protecting you and standing up for our belief in our children not having soda (step 4). I am responsible for letting my mother get away with questioning your judgment. I am also responsible for you feeling torn and alone. I did that to you tonight."

To take responsibility requires some humility. As servants of God and our spouse, we will absolutely make mistakes. These mistakes can hurt those around us. When we make mistakes (not *if* we make mistakes) that harm our spouses, we must take full responsibility with them. By doing so, things can get smoother more quickly rather than over a long time.

5. Ask Them What They Desire from You

Once your spouse feels validated (step 3), and you have taken responsibility (step 4, if applicable), the understanding process is not over. The next step is to stay fully intent on who your spouse is and to ask him or her what he or she desires from you.

After taking responsibility, Charlie might ask Linda, "What do you desire from me or desire I do at this time?" Linda's response might be: "Next time we are together, discuss the soda thing," or, "Call your mom tomorrow—with me present—and share that the soda thing is 'our' belief and that other kids and parents are fine with our decision." She might also say: "Set up a consequence for yourself so that if you do this again, you will feel some 'pain' for this bad choice instead of making me pay for this happening repeatedly."

Stacy might say to Mark: "That's a tough day, no doubt. Is there anything I can do for you?" Mark might say: "Nah, I just needed to vent," or, "A hug, kiss, and iced tea would be great," or, "I might want some time to vent to my brother tonight, if that's okay."

Some challenges that your spouse faces simply need to be met with understanding. There are some circumstances where they might ask something of you. In these cases, even simply offering to be of service is meaningful in many cases.

6. If Reasonable, Do It

When you ask your spouse if they desire something from you (i.e. a hug, kiss, iced tea, or even setting up a consequence), if his or her request is reasonable, go ahead and follow through. Reasonable is what is important here. You cannot self-soothe your spouse or in every situation be able to accomplish the unreasonable.

If someone is asking from the heart, it is usually reasonable. If, however, someone is trying to punish or demean you or seems otherwise unreasonable, you can defer this to a pastor or an accountability couple.

Doing a reasonable thing, if needed, can also validate that you heard your spouse. Serving them in this way in a healthy relationship can be positive. In an unhealthy relationship, "You did me wrong, so here's your punishment," is not the heart of this tool of understanding each other. I recommend counseling if you feel you cannot get through this process together.

7. Practice, Practice, Practice

The understanding skill I just shared must be practiced fourteen to twenty-one times before you are usually qualified to actually use it in your marriage. If you do not practice this skill when your spouse desires to be understood, you will be unable to skillfully be there for them, and you will experience the same old results for years!

This skill is rarely innate in someone, so I recommend you use the following checklist to mark off the dates and topics for when you practiced understanding your spouse. On this checklist you can see a space for the date you practiced, the topic, and the grade for each area.

Understanding Check List

Six Points of Grading

1. Hearing the heart
2. Discovering feelings
3. Validate feelings
4. Take responsibility
5. Ask what he or she desires of you
6. Do it if reasonable

Him #1

Date	Issue	Grade	
		1.	4.
		2.	5.
		3.	6.

Her #1

Date	Issue	Grade	
		1.	4.
		2.	5.
		3.	6.

Him #2

Date	Issue	Grade	
		1.	4.
		2.	5.
		3.	6.

Her #2

Date	Issue	Grade	
		1.	4.
		2.	5.
		3.	6.

Him #3

Date	Issue	Grade	
		1.	4.
		2.	5.
		3.	6.

Her #3

Date	Issue	Grade	
		1.	4.
		2.	5.
		3.	6.

Him #4		
Date	Issue	Grade
		1. 4. 2. 5. 3. 6.

Her #4		
Date	Issue	Grade
		1. 4. 2. 5. 3. 6.

Him #5		
Date	Issue	Grade
		1. 4. 2. 5. 3. 6.

Her #5		
Date	Issue	Grade
		1. 4. 2. 5. 3. 6.

Him #6		
Date	Issue	Grade
		1. 4. 2. 5. 3. 6.

Her #6		
Date	Issue	Grade
		1. 4. 2. 5. 3. 6.

Him #7		
Date	Issue	Grade
		1. 4. 2. 5. 3. 6.

Her #7		
Date	Issue	Grade
		1. 4. 2. 5. 3. 6.

Him #8		
Date	Issue	Grade
		1. 4.
		2. 5.
		3. 6.

Her #8		
Date	Issue	Grade
		1. 4.
		2. 5.
		3. 6.

Him #9		
Date	Issue	Grade
		1. 4.
		2. 5.
		3. 6.

Her #9		
Date	Issue	Grade
		1. 4.
		2. 5.
		3. 6.

Him #10		
Date	Issue	Grade
		1. 4.
		2. 5.
		3. 6.

Her #10		
Date	Issue	Grade
		1. 4.
		2. 5.
		3. 6.

Him #11		
Date	Issue	Grade
		1. 4.
		2. 5.
		3. 6.

Her #11		
Date	Issue	Grade
		1. 4.
		2. 5.
		3. 6.

Him #12		
Date	Issue	Grade
		1. 4. 2. 5. 3. 6.

Her #12		
Date	Issue	Grade
		1. 4. 2. 5. 3. 6.

Him #13		
Date	Issue	Grade
		1. 4. 2. 5. 3. 6.

Her #13		
Date	Issue	Grade
		1. 4. 2. 5. 3. 6.

Him #14		
Date	Issue	Grade
		1. 4. 2. 5. 3. 6.

Her #14		
Date	Issue	Grade
		1. 4. 2. 5. 3. 6.

Him #15		
Date	Issue	Grade
		1. 4. 2. 5. 3. 6.

Her #15		
Date	Issue	Grade
		1. 4. 2. 5. 3. 6.

Him #16

Date	Issue	Grade	
		1.	4.
		2.	5.
		3.	6.

Her #16

Date	Issue	Grade	
		1.	4.
		2.	5.
		3.	6.

Him #17

Date	Issue	Grade	
		1.	4.
		2.	5.
		3.	6.

Her #17

Date	Issue	Grade	
		1.	4.
		2.	5.
		3.	6.

Him #18

Date	Issue	Grade	
		1.	4.
		2.	5.
		3.	6.

Her #18

Date	Issue	Grade	
		1.	4.
		2.	5.
		3.	6.

Him #19

Date	Issue	Grade	
		1.	4.
		2.	5.
		3.	6.

Her #19

Date	Issue	Grade	
		1.	4.
		2.	5.
		3.	6.

Him #20			
Date	Issue	Grade	
		1.	4.
		2.	5.
		3.	6.

Her #20			
Date	Issue	Grade	
		1.	4.
		2.	5.
		3.	6.

Him #21			
Date	Issue	Grade	
		1.	4.
		2.	5.
		3.	6.

Her #21			
Date	Issue	Grade	
		1.	4.
		2.	5.
		3.	6.

"To hear someone's heart is to hear who he or she is."

The Perimeter

Have you ever watched a movie or TV show and heard a cop or soldier speak into his headset to his team, saying, "Secure the perimeter"? Sure you have. Just this past holiday season, Lisa, Hadassah, and I went to see the movie, *Penguins of Madagascar*, in which the head penguin tells the other penguins to "secure the perimeter."

Remember, Adam was first placed in the Garden (a perimeter) and given the responsibility to care for it. Caring for the perimeter was a training ground for Adam to become a servant man. Then he was given Eve, and serving her became part of his job. Sin then entered the world, and ever since leaving the Garden, men have been establishing a perimeter (a home) so they can live and raise a family.

Whether you are a man or woman, ask yourself, *What falls within my perimeter?* Of course, it is the home or apartment you are living in and care for, through maintenance and chores, on a day-to-day basis. If you have children, for sure, they would fall under your perimeter.

(If you are a grandparent, they are within your children's perimeter, but you just get to enjoy them—at least, this is what my friends who are grandparents tell me.) Of course, every perimeter involves the green stuff—not plants or grass—I mean money. This part of the perimeter is vitally important to manage well.

We will also talk about church and friends as part of the perimeter. The perimeter of both your domains involves several areas, all of which change over the course of your servant marriage.

Your perimeter does demand a portion of your life's energy to maintain. If you manage well (and you might need help), then you will have some time left over for that amazing person in your perimeter; your amazing spouse.

Home

To start our discussion on serving in the perimeter, I want to start with the physical house or apartment you live in. Your dwelling place is a gift from God. The size of the house isn't as important as your attitude and cooperation in managing the issues around the house. Now, to be clear, I am talking about the physical place—not the relationships—just the bedrooms, bathrooms, kitchen, etc. When you marry, both spouses have a quite limited set of skills, unless trained in a certain area to deal with drywall, paint, electrical, plumbing, and other types of household repairs.

I will never forget in our first house when the tile in the shower needed to have the grout touched up. My way of solving the problem was to first attempt to fix it. I went to the local Home Depot or Lowes and bought some stuff and a grout gun. I put this round thing in the gun and then squeezed and squeezed, but nothing came out. This went on for over an hour until I realized I was supposed to cut the tip off to grout tube. I laughed afterward, but it really was not funny at the time.

Just a note to the ladies: In general, men do not know how to fix everything any more than you know how to cook everything. Each project has to be taught to us, just as learning to cook requires recipes one can follow.

I am truly surprised that so many couples never really sit down and divvy up specific tasks or responsibilities in the home. It is more common that a system somehow evolves on who does what. There is wisdom in deciding on clearly assigning maintenance issues to secure your perimeter. So, who is responsible for the areas in your dwelling in the chart below?

	Him	Her	Call	Fix
Drywall				
Electrical				
Plumbing				
Appliances				
Heat/Air Conditioning				
Carpets/Flooring				
Light Bulbs				
Door Locks				
Other				

If you take a few minutes and discuss this, you can get an idea of who is responsible for different areas of your home. It really does not matter which person handles what. What does matter is that both spouses agree to get it all done.

I am a get-it-done guy. Lisa has never given me a honey-do list because if I see it and I can do it, it is done. If either of us sees it and it is beyond our skill level, then Lisa usually calls to get it done.

From listening to women talk about their husbands, it seems not all men take on the responsibility of their house as a priority. As men, we are often guilty of being "too busy." I have a saying I live by that goes like this: "Men make a plan; boys make excuses." There may be legitimate reasons to put some things off, and if so, there is usually no tension in the marriage.

Some couples have boundaries set in place as to how long to give a spouse who says he or she is going to fix something—say one week or month. If it is not fixed by the set time, the other person can fix it or call to get it fixed and it is no longer a discussion. They both agreed to the time when a certain thing would be done and the consequence(s) attached.

Getting things fixed can be a place of tension or a place of management. Those in a servant marriage aim at taking responsibility for managing tasks and crises well. Those who are less proactive in management and clear communication can suffer needless tension. If this is an area of weakness, get a mentor couple, partner, or counselor to work out details that allow you both to live in better harmony.

Chores

There are so many little and large ways to serve when you have a dwelling. Yes, oh yes, the countless hours, days, and months of our lives that are consumed with dishes, mopping, vacuuming, cleaning bathrooms, laundry, light bulbs, woodwork, vents, garages, kid's rooms, and so on. As I write this, I have countless memories (as I am sure you do), of doing the same thing again and again.

This reminds me of the scene at the beginning of *The Incredibles,* in which Mr. Incredible is being interviewed and makes a comment about saving the world again. It goes something like this: "I just saved the world again. I wish it would just stay saved. It's like I need to do it again and again. Why can't it just stay saved?"

Chores are a part of life for all of us, throughout our marriage. Some couples settle this issue early in their marriage. Some have systems to see who can do the least and leave the other to do more. Some argue about this for decades, while some peacefully negotiate (though the wealthier among us just have people do various outside and insides chores for us).

Let me give you some creative ideas that some couples have used to revive this very legitimate issue in marriage. Now, remember, we are all servants and serving is a good thing. Now, if what you are doing is already working, still read through some of these ideas so you can share them with your friends as they try to figure it out. These ideas are in no specific order:

1. Write all chores to be done on strips of paper and place in a jar. Whatever chores you pull out, you do.
2. Make a list of chores. Each of you should choose chores you do not mind doing and decide the rest by way of a coin toss.
3. Divide the list into relatively equal amounts of time and rotate the list weekly or monthly.
4. One person does outside house chores. The other does inside house chores.
5. Create a list and work through the list at the same time, each picking one, and keep going until the list is done.
6. One person does it all one week. The other person does it all the next week.
7. Use any idea that works for you both.

Agreeing on chores is actually more important to your servant marriage than the system you come up with to do the chores. If it has been a while since you have had this conversation, I am going to provide a basic list of outside and inside the house chores to facilitate your discussion.

Outside

	He	She	Rotate	Child	Pay Someone
Grass					
Snow removal					
Flower beds					
Bushes					
Painting					
Gutters					
Sprinklers					
Garage					
Automobiles					

Inside

	He	She	Rotate	Child	Pay Someone
Laundry					
Dishes					
Dusting					
Mopping					
Bathrooms					
Changing Sheets					
Kid's Rooms					
Garbage					
Vents/Filters					
Cooking					
Cleaing up after eating					
Vacuuming					
Light bulbs					
Technology (T.V., Computer, Phones)					
Other					
Other					
Other					

Again, it is not as important who does what. You have unique preferences, personalities, work schedules, and more to work with in creating the way the two of you navigate the issue of chores. My only cautions would be: keep it specific, not vague; talk about it; avoid being passive-aggressive; be honest and keep your word, and; in all ways strive to be a trustworthy servant of Christ.

Children

Children are a great blessing from the Lord. We love little baby beings with all of our hearts, almost instantly. There is something in each one of us that would immediately do just about anything for the safety and betterment of our children.

This love is really, really important because it draws us into an extremely different level of sacrifice and service. By the time you think you are doing pretty well as far as being less selfish, children happen. The dying to yourself part takes a quantum leap when you have children.

From the last sentence to this one, I had walked into my son's room. When I turned the light on, two of the light bulbs over his mirror were out. I walked back upstairs to get light bulbs and went back to his room and replaced them. Then I thought my daughter might have a light out as well. I went upstairs to her room and sure enough, over her mirror, she needed a bulb as well. Then I returned to my table to write this for you. Children provide endless opportunities to serve. We get them up, feed them, make sure they finish their homework, pack a different lunch for each, drive them to school, pick them up from school, clean up after their meals, put dishes away, get them to bed—not to mention, we get them to sports, dance, music, or some other amazing activity.

If you have lived through the movie, you definitely get that having children is a call to service that demands slightly more than you have, so you have to depend on God. Children, in addition to needing so much of our energy and time, also create demands on marriage. The chief demand children bring to married couples are all the small daily decisions and overarching decisions on how to raise them.

You both have limited family experience of your own with the family you grew up with, or those of your friends. All parents have strengths and weaknesses, as well as different values, from food to holidays.

You are creating a unique family of your own. There is no perfect family on earth, so do not aim for perfect. Instead, aim for honest, open, warm, godly, goodhearted, or values along those lines. Understanding each other and hearing each other is very important.

Your different genders and personalities, and current cultural trends create enough variables for your parenting to become a unique journey for both of you. Being parents is an extension of being a servant to each other. You will have ample opportunity to grow in serving. Why do you think grandparents are so much more patient? It is because they have had so much selfishness kicked out of them from decades of marriage and raising children that they actually do look and think a lot more like Jesus.

There are no charts in this conversation, just a smile from a fellow traveler, knowing this is a great journey, the journey is for a lifetime, and that there are no known outcomes for any of us on the parenting journey.

Finances

Money is one of the multifaceted things we get to manage and discuss throughout the decades of servant marriage. I believe money is a gift from God and can be a very positive aspect of servant marriage. There are some key issues I have to bring up here so you can navigate finances and be in agreement, at least on the big issues. Once again, the method or system you create is not as important as being in agreement financially.

Tithing

In my office every Monday for at least the past twenty years, I have had a different Christian couple sit in front of me that has come for three or five days to do an intensive and work on their marriage. In our first session, I ask structural questions like how often they date, go out with friends, discuss feelings, pray together, and have sex. The last question I ask is if they fuss or fight about finances or money. Of the many Christian couples I have seen, what do you think 100 percent of the couples who indicate they do have financial issues or difficulties have in common?

Hopefully you guessed it. One hundred percent of Christian couples I have seen for counseling that had financial difficulties did *NOT* tithe. Now, I am a psychologist, not a preacher. I am not going to gain anything from telling you to tithe to your local church. However, as a couple, you will or have already decided whether or not to give at least 10 percent of your income (which comes from God) to your local church, and perhaps to some ministries you believe in.

I have tithed all of my Christian life and I have been blessed financially my whole life. We have taught our children to tithe to the point that, if they forgot their tithe at home, we would go back and get it so they could tithe. I could write a whole book just on the benefits of tithing.

From a marriage perspective, if you have consistent financial difficulties, your marriage is impacted over time with these challenges. I would encourage you to tithe for life, but at least try it for six months and see what God shows you about the blessings of tithing.

Budgeting

Money comes and goes over the course of your marriage. You will probably manage hundreds of thousands of dollars—if not millions—over the decades of being married. How you manage money is also a servant marriage issue.

One of the questions every couple has to address is budgeting. Usually one person is more bent in this direction of budgeting than the other is. In my book, *Intimacy –*

A 100 Day Guide to Lasting Relationships, I write about financial children (adults who want no financial responsibility), financial adolescents (present-minded, pleasure seeking), or financial adults (money is spiritual and needs to be thoughtfully handled). You can see these financial development issues come up when you start talking about budget.

Some couples live abundantly, so they just spend less than they make. However, most couples would be wise to sit down and see what goes in and out and why, and then establish a budget to meet the short-term and long-term goals of the family.

Here is what I would like you to do. Discuss this issue together and get in agreement. If budgeting has been a challenge for your marriage, then find a financial person in your church or another church and be accountable to him or her until your finances are a strength for you.

Savings/Investing/Debt

There are also three other issues you will need to address or avoid in your servant marriage. Just be open and discuss these so you can agree on what you want your position to be as a couple.

My experience of life is that in each stage, you are saving money for the next stage. When you are single, you save for the wedding, then for the house, then for having children, then for your college fund, and then your retirement and medical expenses.

I find those that save for each stage get financially stronger and stronger. Those who do not save seem to get further and further behind and even more dependent as they age. Here are a few options:

1. Pick a percentage you will save regularly and stick to it.
2. Assign a certain income stream to savings.
3. Don't save.

Investing is another issue on which a couple must be in agreement. Now, as American Christians, we are plagued with a false belief we must live on 100 percent of what we make or worse—live beyond what we make (like our government does). Investing is like saving, except you also have to decide what to invest in: stocks, real estate, an annuity, and so on. Once you decide what to invest in, like savings, you decide what percentage you want to invest over time and for what goals. Usually the two purposes for investing are college education and retirement. Each of these should be discussed with financial advisors and accountants so you maximize your tax benefits by how you invest.

Again, agreement is most important as you walk through the issues of investing. It is also very important that both spouses have access to all investing information, investment strategies, and future income.

Debt is one of those not fun discussions couples must have, it is so important to decide. I think it is important that a couple decide what is worth going into debt over and what is not:

	He		She	
	Yes	No	Yes	No
Education				
House				
Car				
Tvs				
Retail Stores				
Boats/ATVs				

In a servant marriage it is really helpful if you are both in agreement on what you are willing to go into debt on. Also, you might want to agree on a percentage of your income that is allowed to service debt (5, 10, 15, or 20). Again, being in agreement on debt can be beneficial as you navigate the financial aspects of your marriage.

Church

Church, I believe, is a vitally important part of establishing perimeters. As Christians, I believe we are called to be a part of the local body of believers and when and how we can serve the local body.

One of the issues to discuss is church attendance. Are we a "Christmas and Easter" marriage? Are we an "attend weekly/bi-weekly, or when we feel like it" marriage? Deciding this together is important. The local church can be a very positive aspect of your servant marriage.

Serving in your local church is also a balancing issue that we need to address as Christians. Serving may ebb and flow over your pre-child years, child years, post child years and grandparenting years. Your gifts individually and as a couple also contribute to this decision.

Again, being in agreement on how or if you serve in a local church, and to what extent and capacity, is important.

Friends

Finally, I want to talk about friends in your servant marriage. Friends influence how you might think, feel, or behave on a variety of issues. Friends role model their values to us over the time we share with them.

Deciding on the filters you have for friendship to be helpful to you as a couple or individual is invaluable. Also, deciding on the time to allot to friends is also important, and will probably change significantly as you go through the various seasons of your servant marriage.

I think friends have value in our life. I am privileged to have a wide range of friends. Lisa and I have a few couples friends as well that we enjoy. So, my encouragement is to have an agreed upon filter for friendship. Make sure you make some time for friends, but keep your marriage a priority.

I hope you enjoyed our little jaunt through serving the perimeters. These perimeters definitely require our service—that is for sure. However, in this perimeter is another calling to service that is even greater than the most magnificent perimeter, and this is the amazing person of our spouse.

"Those in a servant marriage aim at taking responsibility for managing tasks and crises well."

Servant Marriage

The Person

I love talking about the Garden or perimeters God has placed us in. Where you and I live and get to worship Him is truly an amazing place.

However, the creation of our spouse was a whole other level of His creativity and genius. Our spouse, among the billions of people in the world, is unique in so many ways. His or her family experiences, walk with God, friends, education, choices, ambitions, and gifts make him or her, well, him or her.

I believe it is our privilege to, over the course of our entire lives, get to know and learn about the unique creature our spouses are as they evolve throughout our servant marriage. As we have discussed, it is not only our privilege, but our calling to serve them till death do us part.

In the next several pages, I want to highlight some areas of serving one's spouse. My hope is that an idea here or there will prompt you to think or even evaluate your service to your spouse.

I have broken down the area of serving your spouse into several areas. I followed a model of personhood that Paul, through the Holy Spirit, wrote about in 1 Thessalonians 5:23 (NIV):

"May God himself, the God of peace, sanctify you through and through. May your whole spirit, soul and body be kept blameless at the coming of our Lord Jesus Christ."

Your spouse has an amazing spirit, given to him or her by God. This spirit is also given to you by God as a gift. This gift, like so many gifts of God, needs to be personally cared for and maintained by you.

Your spouse has an almost incomprehensible soul. His or her mind, will, and emotions will be under your care and influence for decades. This area of his or her being will also require care from you in a servant marriage.

I will also briefly explore how you can help care for your spouse physically. Their body, like yours, is amazing. But like everything else, his or her body requires regular positive feedings and nurturing to be optimal.

Spirit

Our spouse is above all a spirit being. At the core of him or her is a spirit that best operates if his or spirit is being fed and nourished.

Now, before I talk about your spouse, I want to first talk about you. You are a spirit being as well. Taking care of yourself spiritually is definitely the first order of business to be able to spiritually serve your spouse.

In Romans 1:15 (NIV), Paul says, "That is why I am so eager to preach the gospel..." I cannot serve very well spiritually if I am not spiritually consistent and growing. The reverse happens if a spouse is spiritually weak and inconsistent. He or she will negatively impact your marriage rather than positively impact it.

I said all of this to say that reading your Bible, praying, worshipping and growing spiritually daily and regularly is critical to having a servant marriage. If you do not serve God well, you will be more likely not to serve your spouse well either.

Regular church attendance and meeting regularly with a friend of the same gender is very helpful. When you grow spiritually, everyone in your life benefits.

Your spouse also greatly benefits when you pray together. As a servant, you do not have to worry about this being your personality or not. It is your responsibility to attempt to connect together spiritually. Praying together daily or regularly in the presence of God and God the Father-in-Law is a blessing to Him. I believe He loves being with both of you at the same time as well as individually. He created this trinity of marriage with you both so that He could fellowship and commune with you together. In a servant marriage, your spiritual walk involves both of you together, and not just you as a single man or woman.

Lisa and I have some friends we enjoy individually. However, when we get together with them together, it is a totally different dynamic. I think the Father feels the same way. Remember, marriage is a three-person entity, not just two. Therefore, I encourage you to enjoy the third person in your marriage together on a daily or regular basis.

Beyond praying together, some couples read the Bible together, which is great. When Lisa and I do this, we discuss what we learn for ourselves, *not* what we think the other person *should* be learning or applying.

Spiritual time together is a way for the servant to honor his or her spouse. Some couples do worship together, perhaps by using a worship CD. Some couples read devotions together. Being consistent in spiritual time together is vital for your marriage.

Soul

Spiritual service involves serving your spouse by giving him or her the fruits of the Spirit as we talked about earlier. Remember to stay intentional and have goals for yourselves. Then you will see the benefits in your servant marriage.

The soul of your spouse has been given to you to serve, bless, and support. You are to be part of its healing and growth, standing by them as they take risks, watching them discover their own amazingness.

In Scripture the soul is described as the mind, will, and emotions. Understanding how and why your spouse thinks is a lifelong journey of listening and understanding them. As a servant to your spouse, your ability to serve will be expanded or limited by how well you understand your spouse.

The will alone, however, is not that complicated to understand. The will is simply the ability or choice to be about to persist in a matter. The will can be amazingly strong in persisting through an issue over long periods of time.

That is the easy part of the will for sure. The complicated part of the will is who is actually driving it. When the Spirit of God drives the will, it can be a powerful and beautiful thing to watch. However, the mind might also drive the will. This can be good or bad. If the mind believes a lie, the will can be utilized to drive behavior that confirms the lie. If the will is driven by the truth, the results will be aligned with truth.

Emotions can drive the will as well. In fact, this is by far the most volatile driver of the will. When emotions drive the will, facts and truth can be close at hand or really far away, regardless of which gender you are.

As a servant to your spouse, you want to do your best to know who is driving the will before you engage the will. If you engage the will before having a clear understanding of who is driving at various speeds, you might be more likely to be engaged in a hit and run accident or other incident involving a motor vehicle.

Another aspect of the will that is important to you is to encourage the will when it is operating properly or growing. If your spouse is utilizing their will to learn more, go to school, expand a talent, address difficult issues, build positive relationships, or just get their body back in shape, you want to be their cheerleader.

Your encouragement and praise of them as their spouse can help them believe in themselves. Your praise can also help your spouse take that one more step toward reaching the goal they have set out to reach. Your voice can strengthen or weaken the will of your spouse, depending on whether you serve with praise or poorly by being critical. As a servant toward your spouse, you would do well to strengthen and encourage your spouse to use his or her will to glorify God, the Creator.

Just about every day for the last couple decades or so, Lisa and I have looked each other in the eye (that is important), and told each other two things we appreciate, value, or love most about one another. This makes our marriage a warm place for our hearts to be.

As a servant of your spouse, you will want to learn from him or her how he or she takes course correction in regard to his or her will. Does he or she do it primarily with the Lord, friends of the same gender, through reading more information, by researching his or her family, pastor, or other person of influence. Once you learn this, encourage him or her in the process that works best for him or her.

Lisa is a good example here. She learned early on that I was more internally motivated, so telling me something was not productive at all. She learned to ask me questions to get me to use my brain against myself in a healthy way, and encouraged me to talk to my spiritual male friend when making big decisions.

Some women are injured and offended when their husbands do not hear them, listen to them, or obey them. In my counseling of thousands of men, I have learned that "men make men." Having a man talk to another man can be a healthy way to respectfully nurture his will. I have also seen something similar with women as well. Talking to a woman, she might hear something "new" her husband has been saying for years.

Feelings

Emotions are an interesting part of our humanity. Though they are a significant part of what makes us human, in our culture, there is no place for us to genuinely get trained to identify and communicate feelings with our spouses.

Here I have to digress just for a moment. Remember, I am a psychologist. In the context of marriage counseling I have heard some painful things for sure on how couples are unkind—or worse—abusive to each other.

The last thing you want to do is be spiritually abusive or unkind, even if it is with the best motives or intentions. Jesus was a servant who knew all truth about all people. He used His strength to serve, as we discussed earlier.

I encourage you to read your Bible, spiritual book, or devotional book together with your spouse, however, do not use this time to correct or emphasize something for your spouse to learn. Nobody wants to be bullied spiritually. Here you might want to set a very clear boundary so you share *only* how the teaching applies to you, not your spouse. If someone cannot heed this boundary, it might foster a spirit of dominance, control, or other ill motive that is not truly spiritual.

The person who needs to get control in this area can set a consequence like, "If I start focusing on you during devotions, I will clean the bathrooms." This can put the pain of this inappropriate behavior on the person who is doing it.

In the appendix at the back of this book, there is a list of feelings you can start with to start sharing with your spouse. Make sure you follow the guidelines about not using examples about each other. Be sure to maintain eye contact and do not give each other feedback when sharing your feelings during the exercise.

I have been using this exercise with addicts in their marriages for a very long time. This exercise is found in the book, *The Final Freedom: Pioneering Sexual Addiction Recovery*.

To do the "Feelings Exercise," randomly point to a feeling on the feelings list and put it in the two sentences below.

I feel_____when _____.

I first remember feeling_____when _____
(under the age of 18).

After you do this simple exercise daily for ninety days, two feelings a day, you can experience significant growth in your ability to communicate on an emotional level. After ninety days, you can just do two feelings from your day for the rest of your life and drop the "I first remember feeling..." sentence. Keeping your marriage emotionally regular can guard you from emotionally stuffing and regurgitating negative emotion on each other repeatedly, and allow you to more effectively share healthy, positive feelings. The better emotional skills you both have, the better you can serve one another.

If feelings are a challenge for you, or if one of you struggles with intimacy anorexia, I would strongly recommend my book, *Emotional Fitness*. After about ninety days of doing the exercises in that book, anyone can move from emotionally challenged to having an emotional black belt.

Gifts

I want to take a few minutes to talk to you about the gift of your spouse. If you have kids, as a good parent, you take the gifts of your children very seriously. You realize God gave you that child or children as gift(s), and that each child has several gifts inside his or her little being. That is the way I think it ought to be, at least.

Lisa and I, perhaps like you, have spent incalculable hours on bleachers, pews, grass, or in classrooms and churches watching our children grow in some area of talent (or wannabe talent). However, not every parent invests in his or her child's talent. Lisa and I observed other parents who had the exact opposite view of investing in their children. They had very specific financial goals and saw investing in lessons or sports for their children as a total waste of time and money. Sadly, these parents often denied extremely gifted children an investment from which they could have benefitted tremendously.

You may be old enough to remember the old *Star Trek* series and movies. If not, you are surely aware of the reboot of the series in theaters recently. Regardless of your introduction to *Star Trek* you have been introduced to the main characters, Captain Kirk and Spock.

Captain Kirk did life from his gut, based on hunches and emotion. Spock, on the other hand, used logic to solve conflicts, which at times limited him from solving the crisis at hand. Just like them, in any marriage, one person is better at handling money and the other more or less skilled in emotion. This often due to no fault of either spouse. If your dad did not teach you how to change the oil in your car, you simply did not know how to change oil. However, emotions are part of our everyday life. Learning some basic emotional skills is a great way to serve your marriage.

Lisa and I did this by investing years of our lives (and lots of money) into letting your children experiment with activities and sports. The morning I wrote this, Lisa and I discussed our son, Jubal, and how he played almost every sport during his school years. Our daughter, Hadassah, did cheerleading, piano, teen court and debate in high school. Every summer, Lisa had the children take lessons for something they never tried before: fencing, horseback riding, golf, baseball, tennis, and so on. By doing this, she was trying to let the children experience different activities to see if they had a gift in those areas.

As a parent, you almost instinctively think like this because you want your child to be all that God called him or her to be. As servants toward our spouses, we should be excited to support their gifts.

These are gifts God has given to them. Now, I am not talking about running off and abandoning you and the family. I am talking about within reason, to allow your spouse to explore new things or engage in things they already enjoy.

Lisa and I are recent empty nesters. Lisa has always had a gift for art, throughout her life. When we dated, I remember encouraging her to take art classes and she did amazing work. As we had children, they utilized her talent for art regularly with their projects. Now that the children are gone, Lisa got interested in painting on old windowsills. She is very good at it, so some Saturdays, we shop for old windowsills. As a servant spouse, you want to be aware of your spouse's talents and encourage them to experiment in life with various interests to discover latent talents.

In taking this approach, you may have to invest some time and money, just as you would have for your children. My experience is, it is worth it to see my wife grow and become the woman God wants her to become.

As a couple, you will have to decide how much time or money is appropriate to invest in your own development. This will definitely shift as children become part of your servant marriage and as they leave. Seriously, you might need to get your calendars and phones out to see what is possible. However, I will say that in many of the marriages I have worked with, I have consistently seen one person really likes to learn, grow, adapt, change, educate, and reeducate themselves about one or several topics, while his or her spouse is more bent toward staying the same with no inward desire to grow or change unless a crisis demands such from them.

This is a matter of accepting each other as opposed to trying to change each other. In these circumstances, one person might request more time while the other refuses to evolve. This will take communication and agreement as you celebrate each other's desires.

Body

We are spirit beings with amazing souls, and equally amazing bodies. These bodies are machines that need plenty of maintenance. We get to feed our bodies a few times a day, drink, hopefully exercise, and eventually take showers or baths to keep them maintained.

In this section, I want to first address you. If you are not eating somewhat healthily and exercising moderately, you might be carrying more stress in your body, which can negatively affect your attitude.

When we live a life with stress and do not have a consistent way to de-stress, we will not function optimally. When we exercise, our body and brain can feel a whole lot better, making us better for our marriage.

Just be honest with yourself. If sugar, carbonated drinks, or caffeine are in any way out of control, it can affect your mood and energy. If you are tired all the time or wildly up and down, it is hard for you to be a good servant to your spouse.

Exercise is important for you as well. I have exercised at least a few times a week since my teenage years. When I let stress build in my body, it can change my attitude; I can become short in my communication, selfish, or impatient. When I am consistent with exercise, I feel more balanced and have a little more grace for the bumps of life.

As it relates to your spouse, talk about each of you getting a little consistent time to exercise. This is especially important for the mother who does not take much time for herself. To be a good mother, take some time to care for yourself. The healthier you are the better lover, friend, or parent you will be.

Sex

Sexuality between a husband and wife can be one of the most beautiful, pleasurable experiences in the marriage. The sacredness of sex is awesome and we are privileged to learn and get to know our spouse sexually.

As we did earlier, let me start with you before I get into some powerful ideas about sexuality. First, if you have any roadblocks in the area of sexuality, it is your duty as a sexual servant to heal this area of your being.

I was conceived in adultery, abandoned, sexually abused, addicted to porn and sexual behaviors, and I took full responsibility for recovering from all of it. My perpetrator does not define my sexuality, nor do my bad choices define my sexuality—my God defines my sexuality.

I know better than most that sexual healing is hard work. My God is worth me having done this work, and so is my wife Lisa. She deserves the best I can be.

Hear my heart if you have been sexually abused or raped. Tell a counselor and take a healing journey. I have helped thousands get and stay free from sexual addiction.

If you struggle with sex addiction, get honest immediately and take the steps we outlined earlier so you can heal. If you are simply sexually immature about asking for sex or being sexual, this is your work to do so that you can hear, "Well done good and faithful servant."

I realize that in Christianity overall, we do a less-than-optimal job on the topic of sexuality. If you want more information on this, go to our website. *The Best Sex* DVDs can be helpful as well as the book, *Intimacy: 100-Day Guide to Lasting Relationships.*

I will soon finish a book called, *The 5 Sex Languages*. This will take your sexual skills and learning about each other sexually to an all new level. The following concepts are in the book, *Intimacy: 100-Day Guide to Lasting Relationships.*

The first idea is what I call "3 Tips for a Great Sex Life": Eyes open during sex; some light on so you can see each other, and; nurturing conversation during sex. Do not have silent sex; it can be incomplete and unfulfilling.

Another idea is to create your sexual garden and actually agree on what you are both willing to participate in, without pressure from either spouse.

Finally, create an agreement sexually only if you are already praying together and sharing feelings daily. If these things are not happening, a sexual agreement will not work long-term.

Women truly need spiritual and emotional intimacy so that they feel sexual toward their husbands. Men, focus on intimacy first. Come back after thirty to sixty days of consistent emotional intimacy before making a sexual agreement.

In a sexual agreement, you both initiate sex. If you do not usually ask for sex with words, practice this so you are both confident in asking for sex. Then agree on and establish how many times a week you will have sex. Set up how you want to organize your sex life. Pick days, rotate responsibility every week (or however you can simply understand who is initiating and how often). Finally, set up a consequence if you do not initiate when agreed upon.

As a servant sexually, if you do not grow or get to a place of mutually serving one another, this can become a significant area of stalemate. Sex is not meant to be a place to bully or control the other. That is not about being a servant and would hurt your marriage. If you struggle as a couple or as an individual, I highly recommend qualified help as soon as possible.

Unaddressed sexual issues can lead to the destruction of the quality of your marriage or the marriage itself. Here your spouse only has you.

You determine what type of sexual servant you are: engaged or unengaged, learning or not learning, giving or selfish, secular or godly. If you chose to be an amazing sexual servant along with being an amazing servant in other areas of your marriage, it will cause you to die to yourself and grow toward your spouse.

Understand that nothing I am saying is in any way license for a man or woman to demand or humiliate his or her spouse sexually. To do this is very offensive to the Father-in-Law God who is in the bedroom.

Like most areas of marriage, it is about honor and agreement to love each other in this very sacred way. You both deserve a great sex life and God has given you decades to patiently grow with each other. So, all I have to say is, have fun as you grow sexually together.

Finally

The servant marriage is a lifelong journey with your spouse. This is your calling to serve them, grow toward them, understand them, and behold God in every phase of marriage.

Your service toward your spouse is given to you by God and empowered by His Spirit over your lifetime. He created marriage for you to become Christlike and smile as you begin to look like Him and talk like Him to your spouse.

Servant marriage is a multidimensional journey featuring endless learning about yourself and your spouse. Your trinity together is the ornament God created, from which children grow and are nourished.

My hope is that these pages have been as revolutionary to you as they have been to me, and to many other Christians I have spoken to at conferences. We are all on one journey to hear one thing about our marriage from God: "Well done, good and faithful servant."

"The soul of your spouse has been given to you to serve, bless, and support."

Appendix

Feelings List

1. I feel (put word here) when (put a present situation when you feel this).
2. I first remember feeling (put the same feeling word here) when (explain earliest occurrence of this feeling).

Rules For Couples: 1- No examples about each other or the relationship. 2-Eye contact. 3-No feedback

Abandoned	Aware	Close	Deprived	Feisty
Abused	Awestruck	Cold	Deserted	Ferocious
Aching	Badgered	Comfortable	Desirable	Foolish
Accepted	Baited	Comforted	Desired	Forced
Accused	Bashful	Competent	Despair	Forceful
Accepting	Battered	Competitive	Despondent	Forgiven
Admired	Beaten	Complacent	Destroyed	Forgotten
Adored	Beautiful	Complete	Different	Free
Adventurous	Belligerent	Confident	Dirty	Friendly
Affectionate	Belittled	Confused	Disenchanted	Frightened
Agony	Bereaved	Considerate	Disgusted	Frustrated
Alienated	Betrayed	Consumed	Disinterested	Full
Aloof	Bewildered	Content	Dispirited	Funny
Aggravated	Blamed	Cool	Distressed	Furious
Agreeable	Blaming	Courageous	Distrustful	Gay
Aggressive	Bonded	Courteous	Distrusted	Generous
Alive	Bored	Coy	Disturbed	Grouchy
Alone	Bothered	Crabby	Dominated	Grumpy
Alluring	Brave	Cranky	Domineering	Hard
Amazed	Breathless	Crazy	Doomed	Harried
Amused	Bristling	Creative	Doubtful	Hassled
Angry	Broken-up	Critical	Dreadful	Healthy
Anguished	Bruised	Criticized	Eager	Helpful
Annoyed	Bubbly	Cross	Ecstatic	Helpless
Anxious	Burdened	Crushed	Edgy	Hesitant
Apart	Burned	Cuddly	Edified	High
Apathetic	Callous	Curious	Elated	Hollow
Apologetic	Calm	Cut	Embarrassed	Honest
Appreciated	Capable	Damned	Empowered	Hopeful
Appreciative	Captivated	Dangerous	Empty	Hopeless
Apprehensive	Carefree	Daring	Enraged	Horrified
Appropriate	Careful	Dead	Enraptured	Hostile
Approved	Careless	Deceived	Enthusiastic	Humiliated
Argumentative	Caring	Deceptive	Enticed	Hurried
Aroused	Cautious	Defensive	Esteemed	Hurt
Astonished	Certain	Delicate	Exasperated	Hyper
Assertive	Chased	Delighted	Excited	Ignorant
Attached	Cheated	Demeaned	Exhilarated	Joyous
Attacked	Cheerful	Demoralized	Exposed	Lively
Attentive	Childlike	Dependent	Fake	Lonely
Attractive	Choked Up	Depressed	Fascinated	Loose

Lost	Pulled apart	Sexy	Tight	Whole
Loving	Put down	Shattered	Timid	Wicked
Low	Puzzled	Shocked	Tired	Wild
Lucky	Quarrelsome	Shot down	Tolerant	Willing
Lustful	Queer	Shy	Tormented	Wiped out
Mad	Quiet	Sickened	Torn	Wishful
Maudlin	Raped	Silly	Tortured	Withdrawn
Malicious	Ravished	Sincere	Touched	Wonderful
Mean	Ravishing	Sinking	Trapped	Worried
Miserable	Real	Smart	Tremendous	Worthy
Misundertstood	Refreshed	Smothered	Tricked	
Moody	Regretful	Smug	Trusted	
Morose	Rejected	Sneaky	Trustful	
Mournful	Rejuvenated	Snowed	Trusting	
Mystified	Rejecting	Soft	Ugly	
Nasty	Relaxed	Solid	Unacceptable	
Nervous	Relieved	Solitary	Unapproachable	
Nice	Remarkable	Sorry	Unaware	
Numb	Remembered	Spacey	Uncertain	
Nurtured	Removed	Special	Uncomfortable	
Nuts	Repulsed	Spiteful	Under control	
Obsessed	Repulsive	Spontaneous	Understanding	
Offended	Resentful	Squelched	Understood	
Open	Resistant	Starved	Undesirable	
Ornery	Responsible	Stiff	Unfriendly	
Out of control	Responsive	Stimulated	Ungrateful	
Overcome	Repressed	Stifled	Unified	
Overjoyed	Respected	Strangled	Unhappy	
Overpowered	Restless	Strong	Unimpressed	
Overwhelmed	Revolved	Stubborn	Unsafe	
Pampered	Riled	Stuck	Unstable	
Panicked	Rotten	Stunned	Upset	
Paralyzed	Ruined	Stupid	Uptight	
Paranoid	Sad	Subdued	Used	
Patient	Safe	Submissive	Useful	
Peaceful	Satiated	Successful	Useless	
Pensive	Satisfied	Suffocated	Unworthy	
Perceptive	Scared	Sure	Validated	
Perturbed	Scolded	Sweet	Valuable	
Phony	Scorned	Sympathy	Valued	
Pleasant	Scrutinized	Tainted	Victorious	
Pleased	Secure	Tearful	Violated	
Positive	Seduced	Tender	Violent	
Powerless	Seductive	Tense	Voluptuous	
Present	Self-centered	Terrific	Vulnerable	
Precious	Self-conscious	Terrified	Warm	
Pressured	Selfish	Thrilled	Wary	
Pretty	Separated	Ticked	Weak	
Proud	Sensuous	Tickled	Whipped	

Guideline #1:
No Examples
About Each Other

Guideline #2:
Maintain Eye
Contact

Guideline #3:
No Feedback

MARRIAGE

This 100 Day guide can transform couples from any level of intimacy to a lifestyle of satiation with their spouse. $11.99

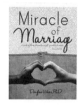

Just like every child has a DNA and destiny, so does your one-of-a-kind miracle called marriage. Dr. Weiss walks you through the creation and maintenance of your marriage. $12.95

Christ wants you to have a great marriage and this DVD set is just another avenue in obtaining your miracle of marriage. $29.95

This book helps develop faithfulness, patience, forgiveness, service, respect, kindness, and celebration, all of which contribute to an exciting, loving and wonderful relationship. $13.99

By taking ten minutes a day to focus on each other, you can enhance your marriage in ways you'll appreciate for a lifetime. $14.99

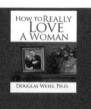

In this 12 part DVD series, you will be exposed to tried and true principles to help you learn how to really love a woman. $69.00

30-Day Marriage Makeover shows you how to energize your relationship and create the intimacy that you long for. $16.99

These DVD are a must for every Christian men and woman. You are practically and passionately walked through Christian sexuality that really works. $29.95(each)

Everyone has an unlimited number of emotions, but few have been trained to identify, choose, communicate, and master them. $16.95

INTIMACY ANOREXIA

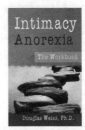

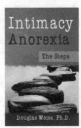

This hidden addiction is destroying so many marriages today. In your hands is the first antidote for a person or spouse with anorexia to turn the pages on this addiction process. $22.95

This is like therapy in a box. Inside is 100 exercises that have already been proven helpful in treating intimacy anorexia. $39.95

This is the only twelve step workbook just for intimacy anorexia. Each step gives you progress in your healing from intimacy anorexia. $14.95

This book will not only unlock the understanding of intimacy anorexia but you will also hear experiences of spouses who have found themselves married and alone. $14.95

This is the first workbook to offer practical suggestions and techniques to better navigate through recovery from your spouse's Intimacy Anorexia. $39.95

These Steps can further your healing and recovery from your spouse's Intimacy Anorexia. $14.95

This DVD will give you the characteristics, causes and strategies of intimacy anorexia. This DVD also provides solutions for the intimacy anorexic to start their road to recovery. $69.95

This DVD is for the spouse of an intimacy/sexual anorexic. Dr. Weiss will help you to start a journey of recovery from living with a spouse with intimacy anorexia. $49.95

MEN'S RECOVERY

This book gives more current information than many professional counselors have today on sexual addiction. $22.95

This workbook will outline the best techniques to help obtain freedom from sexual addiction. $39.95

This step book is specifically written for the person desiring recovery from sexual addiction. $14.95

Offers practical tools for hearing her pain, navigating her grief and losses, discovering her expectations of you and the boundaries she may need to heal. $89.95

This CD will give you more information than most therapists have on sexual addiction. You will be able to finally know how you became a sexual addict and identify why you might still be relapsing. $29.95

Once you know the type of sex addict you are, Dr. Doug outlines the same treatment plan you would receive in an individual session. $29.95

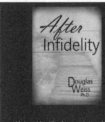

Helps identify key points about the whys of infidelity, the types of cheaters, and how to start walking toward a healthy marriage. $49.95

This amazing DVD has 8 addicts telling their stories through directed questions. These individuals address key issues along with their journey through recovery. $19.95

Making Amends was created for men who are working through their sexual addiction recovery and have reached Step 9 where they make amends to their wife. $19.95

WOMEN'S RECOVERY

This book offers the readers hope, along with a plan for recovery. Any woman who is a partner of a sex addict will find this book a necessity for her journey toward healing. $14.95

This is like therapy in a box for women who want to walk through the residual effects of being in a relationship with a sex addict. $39.95

This is an interactive workbook that allows the partners of sex addicts to gain insight and strength through working the Twelve Steps. $14.95

This DVD set is for any woman who is currently or was in a relationship with a sexual addict. If anger is still an issue, this material can help with her healing. $29.95

In this DVD set Dr. Weiss will expose the viewer to specific reasons as to why men lie and helpful strategies to end the lying. $44.95

In 90-minutes, this DVD answers the ten most frequently asked questions for partners of sex addicts. $69.95

This amazing DVD has 8 partners of sex addicts telling their stories through directed questions. A must DVD for every spouse of a sex addict. $19.95

This 2 hour DVD set was produced for divorced women who desire to date again. $29.95

This book answers these questions in a new way that makes sense for those who commit adultery and those who are impacted by the behavior. $14.95

OTHER RESOURCES

"Born for War" teaches practical tools to defeat these sexual landmines and offers scriptural truths that empower young men to desire successfulness in the war thrust upon them. $29.95

This 2 hour DVD helps single women ages 15-30, to successfully navigate through the season of dating. $29.95

This 2 Disc DVD Series is definitely nothing you have heard before. Dr. Weiss charts new territory as to the why for sexual purity. $29.95

A gift for your daugher as she enters college. Letters to my Daughter includes my daily letters to my daughter during her first year of college. $14.95

Erin discovers she comes from a long line of dragons, dragons who have effectively maintained Earth's balance since the planet's beginning. Will she accept her fate and responsibility? $14.95

Within these pages of this book you will find a tried and true path for recovery from any addiction. Here you will get a biblical understanding to break the strongholds in your life forever. $22.95

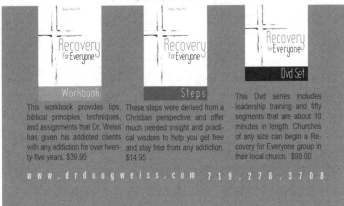

This workbook provides tips, biblical principles, techniques, and assignments that Dr. Weiss has given his addicted clients with any addiction for over twenty-five years. $39.95

These steps were derived from a Christian perspective and offer much needed insight and practical wisdom to help you get free and stay free from any addiction. $14.95

This Dvd series includes leadership training and fifty segments that are about 10 minutes in length. Churches of any size can begin a Recovery for Everyone group in their local church. $99.00

www.drdougweiss.com 719.278.3708

CLEAN RESOURCES

Every Christian man is born into a sexual war. The enemy attacks the young, hoping to scar them permanently and leave them ruined. But your past is not enough to keep you from the enduringly clean life you want and deserve. $16.99

This journal is designed to be used in conjunction with the Clean book and the Clean DVD set. This set can be used individually or in a church small group or accountability group. $14.99

This DVD set exposes you to many tried and true spiritual truths with very practical applications. You and your church are about to take an amazing journey towards God's insights for your freedom. $29.99

LUST FREE RESOURCES

Every man can fight for and obtain a lust free lifestyle. Once you know how to stop lust, you will realize how weak lust really can be. God gave you the power to protect those you love from the ravages of lust for the rest of your life! It's time to take it back! $13.95

This DVD series walks you through how every man can fight for and obtain a lust free lifestyle. Once you know how to stop lust, you will realize how weak lust really can be. God gave you the power to protect those you love from the ravages of lust for the rest of your life! It's time to take it back! $23.95

>>>>>>>>>>>>>>>>> STAY CONNECTED

5080 MARK DABLING BOULEVARD., COLORARDO SPRINGS, COLORADO 80918 > 719.278.3708 > HEART2HEART@XC.ORG

- in LINKEDIN.COM/IN/DOUGLASWEISSPUD
- f FACEBOOK.COM/DOUGLAS.WEISS.18
- 🐦 TWITTER.COM/DRDOUGWEISS
- ☁ SOUNDCLOUD.COM/DRDOUGWEISS
- Ⓦ DRDOUGWEISS.COM/BLOG
- 🅰 "DR. DOUGS TIPS" FROM APP STORE
- Ⓥ VIMEO.COM/DOUGLASWEISS
- ▶ YOUTUBE.COM/C/DOUGLASWEISS
- Ⓟ PINTEREST.COM/DOUGLASWEISS
- 📷 INSTAGRAM.COM/DRDOUGWEISS

SUBSCRIBE TO OUR WEEKLY NEWSLETTERS AT DRDOUGWEISS.COM   MARRIAGE TIPS   RECOVERY TIPS   PARTNER TIPS

COUNSELING

"Without the intensive, my marriage would have ended and I would not have known why. Now I am happier than ever and my marriage is bonded permanently."

Counseling Sessions

Couples are helped through critical phases of disclosure moving into the process of recovery, and rebuilding trust in relationships. We have helped many couples rebuild their relationship and grasp and implement the necessary skills for an intimate relationship.

Individual counseling offers a personal treatment plan for successful healing in your life. In just one session a counselor can help you understand how you became stuck and how to move toward freedom.

Partners of sex addicts need an advocate. Feelings of fear, hurt, anger, betrayal, and grief require a compassionate, effective response. We provide that expert guidance and direction. We have helped many partners heal through sessions that get them answers to their many questions including: "How can I trust him again?"

A counseling session today can begin your personal journey toward healing.

3 and 5 Day Intensives

in Colorado Springs, Colorado
are available for the following issues:

- Sexual Addiction Couple or Individual
- Marriage Intensives
- Partners of Sexual Addicts
- Intimacy Anorexia
- Victims of Sexual Abuse
- Adult Children of Sex Addicts
- Teenage Children of Sex Addicts
- Teen Intensive

Attendees of Intensives will receive:

- Personal attention from counselors who specialize in your area of need
- An understanding of how the addiction /anorexia and its consequences came into being
- Three appointments daily
- Daily assignments to increase the productiveness of these daily sessions
- Individuals get effective counseling to recover from the effects of sexual addiction, abuse and anorexia
- Addiction, abuse, anorexia issues are thoroughly addressed for couples and individuals. This includes the effects on the partner or family members of the addict, and how to rebuild intimacy toward a stronger relationship.

CONFERENCES

What an incredible way to deliver such a sensitive, "hush hush" topic!! Thank you from the bottom of my heart. I really enjoyed tonight's conference. Today will count as the first day of my sexual sobriety.

CLEAN
is a powerful men's conference equipping men to join the battle to maintain sexual purity. In this conference, men will be given tools and biblical principles so they can get started immediately.

PURITY
Mixed audiences can be impacted by Successfully Single, as well as Born for War for Male Teens and Princes take Longer than Frogs for Female Teens to help motivate them to fight for their sexual purity.

MEN
The Sex, Men & God conferences is where men experience great personal growth and understanding into their sexuality...where other speakers rarely go. How to Really Love a Woman is really practical training for the men in your church.

COUPLES
attending the Intimacy, 10 Minute Marriage or The 7 Love Agreements Conference discover how to discuss their desires, learn the importance of marital dating, how to connect emotionally, how to let go of your past and much more.

WOMEN
How to Really Love a Man and Best Sex for Women are great inspiring and practical teachings for the women in your church.

For additional conference information, including available dates, please call our office at 719-278-3708, visit our website at www.drdougweiss.org or you may also email us at conferences@drdougweiss.org